122
123
127
135

35 - 39

EUGENE GLADSTONE O'NEILL
1888-1953

This informal picture
was taken in 1938.

EUGENE O'NEILL

THE MAN
AND
HIS PLAYS

Barrett H. Clark

DOVER PUBLICATIONS, INC.
NEW YORK

This Dover edition, first published in 1947, is a
revised and enlarged version of the work published
by Robert M. McBride & Company in 1929.

An Addenda listing the first production and publication of Eugene O'Neill's plays from 1947 to 1966
was added to the Dover Edition in 1967.

Standard Book Number: 486-20379-4
Library of Congress Catalog Card Number: 47-31325

Manufactured in the United States of America
Dover Publications, Inc.
180 Varick Street
New York, N. Y. 10014

PREFACE

IN 1926 I published a 100-page book for the Modern American Writers series; this was issued by Robert M. McBride and Company in New York under the title *Eugene O'Neill*. The next year the book was re-issued, with changes, for distribution to audiences ("free with each orchestra seat") who attended a revival of *Beyond the Horizon*. In 1929 it was drastically revised and brought up to date, under the McBride imprint, bearing the title *Eugene O'Neill the Man and His Plays*. The book was again revised to some extent in 1933 and issued as a text-book, still under the McBride ægis. In 1933, also, it was slightly revised and published in London by Jonathan Cape Ltd. Further revisions were made and new material added, and in 1936 McBride brought out another edition. In the early 1940's the book went out of print and because of wartime shortages it was not re-issued. In 1945 the latest edition was translated into Spanish by Manuel Barberá and published by Editorial Nova in Buenos Aires. The original text was slightly expanded for this edition and a short chapter added. A translation into Greek has been made by Basil Nicolopoulos, translator of several of O'Neill's plays, and will be published in Athens in 1947.

The present volume, though based to some extent on the earlier books just mentioned, is virtually a new work. Except for the quotations from letters, articles and plays, every page of the text has been re-written. A great deal of new material has been added, both my own, and that of others. I have been careful to give due credit to persons, periodicals and publishing firms whose written and spoken utterances are here used, but I should like to emphasize in this place my particular obligations to Mr. O'Neill himself, to Mrs. Carlotta Monterey O'Neill; to the publishers Boni and Liveright (later Liveright, Inc.) and to Random House (O'Neill's present publishers) for leave to reprint excerpts from the plays; to Saxe Commins of Random House for like permission and for personal favors; to Maxwell Perkins of Charles Scribner's Sons for permission to examine the Wilderness Edition of O'Neill; to Joseph Heidt of the Theatre Guild; to George Jean Nathan, for reasons that will appear in the book; to Ralph Sanborn, co-author with me of *A Bibliography of the Works of Eugene O'Neill*, and author of the Check List which appears at the end of the present volume; and to a great many others whose names will appear in their proper places in the pages that follow.

The frontispiece of O'Neill in this book was taken by the late Harry Weinberger, O'Neill's friend and attorney for many years. It has never before been published.

CONTENTS

THE MAN

Hotel Lafayette, 1926   3

Getting Him to Sit for His Portrait   5

Autobiography   9

He Is Born   11

The First Voyage   14

Jimmy the Priest's   16

Barnstorming   17

He Becomes a Reporter   18

Illness   20

Discharged as Arrested   21

The Turning Point   22

He Goes to Harvard   25

Provincetown   29

"Jig" Cook   31

The Thirst Volume   33

First Production—Bound East for Cardiff   34

The Provincetown Players   35

The Smart Set and Its Editors   37

Trying to Sell Plays   38

Leading Dramatist   38

Drinking   42

A "Colyum" Poet   43

THE PLAYS

The Earliest Plays 49

Thirst and Other Plays 49

Experiment 53

The Moon of the Caribbees and Other One-Acters 56

The Background of the Sea Plays 58

O'Neill on the Sea Plays 58

Before Breakfast and The Dreamy Kid 63

Beyond the Horizon 65

Chris Christopherson 68

The Straw 69

The Emperor Jones 71

The Failure of Gold 73

An Austrian Poet on O'Neill 75

Anna Christie 75

Diff'rent 79

Murder and Suicide 81

The Quest for New Forms 81

The Hairy Ape 82

Foreign Influences 83

Supernaturalism 86

The First Man 87

Welded and The Problem of Marriage 90

All God's Chillun Got Wings 93

A New Note in Tragedy—Desire Under the Elms 96

Desire and the Censors 97

Transition Experiments and The Fountain 100

The Ancient Mariner 102

Symbolism and The Great God Brown 103

Marco Millions 107

Strange Interlude 111

Lazarus Laughed   116
Dynamo   119
Mourning Becomes Electra   122
Ah, Wilderness!   137
Days Without End   139
TEMPORARY RETIREMENT, 1934–1946   142
The Iceman Cometh   154
IN MID-CAREER   159
A Moon for the Misbegotten   162

BIBLIOGRAPHY
FIRST PRODUCTIONS OF PLAYS   165
CHECK-LIST OF THE FIRST PUBLICATION OF THE
    PLAYS, BY RALPH SANBORN   167
INDEX TO SAME, BY RALPH SANBORN   170
PUBLISHED LETTERS, ARTICLES, NOTES, ETC. BY
    O'NEILL   171
SELECTED READING LIST ON O'NEILL   172
ADDENDA: 1947-1966   178

INDEX   180

The Provincetown Players

April 26, 27, 28, 29, 30, May 1,2

THE HERMIT AND HIS MESSIAH

A Play by F. B. Kugelman

The Hermit ....George Cram Cook
The Spy ....Samuel Eliot, Jr.

Produced by the Actors.
Scene designed and executed by
Flossette Florence Heaton

THE ROPE

A Play by Eugene G. O'Neill

Abraham Bentley.......................O. K. Liveright
Annie, His Daughter..................Dorothy Upjohn
Pat Sweeney, Her Husband............H. B. Tisdale
Mary, Their Child.......................Edna Smith
Luke Bentley, Abe's Son by a Second Marriage,
Charles Ellis

Place: An Old Barn
Time: Today
Directed by Nina Moise

WOMAN'S HONOR

A Comedy by Susan Glaspell

Mr. Foster, The Lawyer.................Justus Sheffield
Gordon Wallace. The Prisoner............Clark Branyon
Boy ....Murray Cooper

The Shielded One		Marjory Lacey
The Motherly One		Dorothy Upjohn
The Scornful One	The Women	Ida Rauh
The Silly One		Norma Millay
The Mercenary One		Alice MacDougal
The Cheated One		Susan Glaspell

Place: A Room in the Sheriff's House.
Directed by Nina Moise and Susan Glaspell.

Program for *The Rope*, forerunner of *Desire Under the Elms*
and *The Iceman Cometh*. New York, 1918.

A SHY and silent young man in a brown well-fitting home-spun suit, tall, thin, a little angular, sits uneasily on a gilt chair before a closed writing-desk in a large dark room. Scene, the Hotel Lafayette, New York City. Through the heavy lace curtains is a row of dingy houses across University Place. It is raining. The lank brown figure rises and smilingly offers me a place on the sofa, then crosses and perches on the edge of the wide old-fashioned brass bed. His face is narrow, his forehead high; the black hair is slightly tinged with white at the temples; the eyes are clear, bright and penetrating, yet infinitely soft. The black close-trimmed moustache emphasizes the severity of the straight wide mouth.

He begins to speak—slowly, hesitatingly, reluctantly. He gets up and goes to the window, crosses back, hitching up his belt on the way. Then poising himself carefully once more on the edge of the bed he quickly eats his frugal luncheon, which a waiter has just brought up from the kitchen. After a brief silence he again begins to speak, and the words come more easily, as though the resonance of his musical voice were marshalling the phrases and sentences and coaxing them from the depths.

He smiles; I smile. We have met before, and before that we have corresponded and talked at length by telephone, but this time it is harder to begin. It seems even a little absurd, doesn't it? O'Neill is just thirty-eight, and I a year younger. I have come here ostensibly to chat with him about the theater of the past, the present, and the future, but it is my real business to discuss in detail this matter of writing about him. I am uneasy and self-conscious, and I think he is, too. I've been invited to write a book about this young man, but the young

3

man feels he has hardly got into his stride. A book! Already! He wonders if it's necessary to be so darned personal about it? His life belongs to himself, doesn't it? Surely I'll have enough material if I stick to the plays, and leave the man out of the picture?

No, I can't do that. The man is a part of the whole thing.— A long pause—a wry smile.

Personal accounts of the young playwright have already crept into print, several lies and exaggerations; a lot of legendary anecdotes are going the rounds, and there will surely be more.

Well—

Once again the wry smile. He must face the situation. If I don't do the job, someone else will, so we had better get the facts straight right now. Very well, but let's not either of us take the thing too seriously. If some kind of book must be written, the ground has got to be cleared. He tries to help; he gives me a sober account of some apocryphal legend, but thinks it best for me to go to other people for an outline of his life. When the MS. is ready he will look it over. He'll tell me what I haven't been able to learn from anyone else. How about it? Another pause. So that's that, and for the rest of the afternoon we talk about *Desire Under the Elms* and *The Fountain*, the Provincetown Players, plans for new plays to be written next year, and the year after that, but mostly about *The Great God Brown*. I have had the MS. with me for the past week and as he takes it he asks how I like it. He stands by the window now, cigarette in hand, eyes fixed on me as though at the moment he were really interested in what I thought of the new play. He listens intently, a thin wave of smoke curling between his fingers.—I have told him what I thought without interruption.

He pulls out his watch and apologizes for having to go so soon. He musically murmurs that he's late for rehearsal. Won't I come with him to the theater? It's just a couple of minutes away? Wait a second—

Stalking to the bathroom, he opens the wall cabinet, carefully measures the ingredients from a couple of bottles in a small cup and mixes a tumblerful of medicine. Drinking it off, he comes back to the table and stuffs a worn copy of Nietzsche's *Birth of Tragedy* into his coat pocket, and we feel our way down the side stairs and out into the street. Our taxi skids over to the Greenwich Village Theatre. . . .

This happened some twenty-one years ago. The MS. of my little monograph was passed on by O'Neill (with alterations and additions), and the volume appeared in the fall of 1926.

I next saw O'Neill after his return from Bermuda with the finished MS. of *Lazarus Laughed*, an early draft of *Strange Interlude*, and a headful of ideas.

GETTING HIM TO SIT FOR HIS PORTRAIT

WHEN this work was first undertaken, I had intended to offer in a few introductory pages a simple statement of the facts of his life, take my notes to O'Neill and have the finished product certified by him as historically correct.

But the subject of my study could not be so lightly disposed of. The more I saw of him and the more I bothered his friends for their impressions, the more difficult did this particular job of describing the man become.

An intelligible discussion of his plays must be based on some knowledge of their origin during the years when, however tentatively or experimentally, he was trying to find a meaning in life; when, like Synge, he was seeking all that had edge, "all that is salt in the mouth, all that is rough to the hand, all that heightens the emotions by contest, all that stings into life the sense of tragedy."

My earliest impression remains substantially what it was the first day I laid eyes on him. He is tall and slender and wiry, with long arms and strong hands. His body is lithe and might be thought awkward if it were not under perfect control. He is shy and diffident; he usually seems embarrassed; unless he is discussing what interests him, he speaks haltingly or not at all. His silences are long and eloquent. His face in repose has a chiselled but by no means cold severity; his smile is disarmingly frank and engaging. There is something at times almost impish in his low-toned comments, which are apt to be tinged with gleeful malice that's more a manner of talking than an expression of opinion. With the ordinary amenities of social intercourse he has no patience, yet no one would dream of calling him discourteous. What interests him and awakens his sympathy and imagination engrosses all his attentive faculties; what does not passes by without seeming to make the slightest impression.

He is fundamentally a passionate observer of humanity, a man to whom life is a tragic, exciting and beautiful adventure; a theatrical craftsman of compelling power; an artist in intent even in his failures; an uncompromising idealist.

Here is what he wrote in 1925 in answer to a letter of mine telling of the publishers' suggestion that I should do a book about him:

"Frankly, I honestly don't believe that I deserve any book —as yet! It seems to me there is too damn much of that premature sort of thing being done in America. On the other hand, if it's got to be done—" In putting the matter before O'Neill I had already told him I agreed with his contention, and thought it foolish to get out an "official" biography; that would, indeed, be premature. He is still growing, mentally, philosophically, artistically, and I can detect in him no sign of any hardening of the creative arteries. In spite of his long and protracted illnesses—particularly during the 1934 to 1946 period—I find him more intellectually alert, more ambitious to undertake difficult labors, less willing to take it easy, and far more interested in the world about him, than ever before. His eagerness to explore new fields and try new forms has taken on gigantic proportions. To attempt any summing up of the man's life work would of course be premature: he is so intensely alive and restless there is no telling what he will do next, nor how far he will go.

Yet it was inevitable that books should be written about him. I pointed this out in my answer to the letter I just quoted, and added that I would attempt no formal study, only a sketch, an account of work already accomplished; there would be no scholarly documentation; no attempt to "place" the subject and his work in any literary pigeonhole. I would do my best not to make him look foolish as a man or a playwright.

Before my first conference with him I had collected a mass of material, making detailed notes on what I had been able to get from his friends and associates, and from articles and interviews published in newspapers and magazines. O'Neill went over this carefully, and pointed out that while my facts were on the whole accurate, the total impression was by no means what it should be. Several of my picturesque anecdotes were apocryphal, and I had failed to present a three-dimensional likeness. Only he put it more tactfully.

In returning my first draft he wrote:

"It seems to repeat somehow, to need cutting—this in addition to the marks I have taken the liberty to make on it by way of suggestion and criticism. You will find a lot of these. You see, when you speak in the script of my having helped on the details of it, you make me a bit responsible, so I've waded right in, even to the extent of suggesting word changes which I thought better expressed the truth. . . . When all is said and done—and this is, naturally, no conceivable fault of yours—the result of this first part is legend. It isn't really true. It isn't I. And the truth would make such a much more interesting—and incredible!—legend. That is what makes me melancholy. But I see no hope for this except some day to shame the devil myself, if I ever can muster the requisite interest—and nerve—simultaneously! The trouble with anyone else writing even a sketch is that I don't believe there is anyone alive today [1926] who knew me intimately in more

than one phase of a life that has passed through many entirely
distinct periods, with complete changes of environment, associates, etc. And I myself might not be so good at writing it;
for when my memory brings back this picture or episode or
that one, I simply cannot recognize that person in myself nor
understand him nor his acts as mine (though objectively I
can), although my reason tells me he was undeniably I.''

In 1933 Mrs. Carlotta Monterey O'Neill told me that she
had discussed with her husband the anecdotes I had picked
up from time to time. She had had "quite a talk about these
things, and I begged him to take the time some day and go
over them with you, straightening out the anecdotes, putting
truth in them! He said, 'Nonsense, what do I care what they
say—the further from the truth they have it, the more privacy I have! It's like a mask!' To which I replied, 'I don't
mind, either, except that they make these so-called legends so
silly and hoodlumish, whereas the true story would be gayer,
more you, and the truth—even if not so nice!' " And she
added, "He will never tell the truth about himself, because
in so doing he would have to tell the truth about others close
to him . . . and that would involve others!"

What O'Neill wrote in his letter quoted above applied only
to the biographical section. As to the criticism—the greater
part of the MS.—he thought otherwise: "Not that I agree
with you at all points where you take exception—or where
you praise. There is plenty I would like to argue with you
about." In other words, the early study which grew into the
book that first appeared in 1926, and in revised form was
re-issued in 1929, 1933, and 1936, was "official," and while he
checked the biographical facts he had nothing to do with
any critical judgment I passed on the plays.

Later interviews and many letters helped me materially in
collecting the available facts. I got in touch with as many of
O'Neill's friends as I could find, and in the course of my
narrative I believe I have given each of them due credit.

Among those who have taken the trouble to tell me much that has never been in print (with some that never will be) are Judge Frederick P. Latimer, former editor of the New London *Telegraph;* Charles Webster, who acted with Eugene in his father's company; Edna Kenton, associated with the Provincetown Players during the early days; Harry Kemp, Edward J. Ballantine, M. Eleanor Fitzgerald, James Light, Charles O'Brien Kennedy, and Richard J. Madden. Frank Shay has told me wonderful tales of human interest. For various matters of fact I am indebted to Kenneth Macgowan, Alfred Kreymborg, George Jean Nathan, the late Professor George P. Baker, Susan Glaspell, Jasper Deeter, and Manuel Komroff. The late Dr. Isaac Goldberg has allowed me to use some of the O'Neill letters to George Nathan, printed in his *Theatre of George Jean Nathan,* and Horace Liveright has made it possible to reprint passages from the plays. (Random House took over the publishing rights from Liveright, and to that firm I am indebted for the privilege of using excerpts from both the early plays and the later ones.) Members of the Theatre Guild staff have helped me considerably, and Clara Weiss, formerly of the Greenwich Village Theatre, has passed on to me programs, clippings and other material. Similar service has more recently been rendered by M. Eleanor Fitzgerald, Susan Glaspell, and Helen Deutsch, co-author with Stella Hanau of the entertaining and informative book, *The Provincetown, A Story of the Theatre.*

Other sources drawn upon—books and articles and programs—are listed at the end of this volume. For the critical opinions I alone am, of course, answerable.

AUTOBIOGRAPHY

EARLY in 1919 O'Neill sent me a short autobiographical note, for use in an article of mine which appeared in the New York *Sun* (May 18), the first, I think, to deal broadly with the man's achievements as a writer. He said:

"Your letter is encouragement of a deeply appreciated kind, and I am sincerely grateful for the renewed confidence with which it heartens me. Your sympathetic interest could not fail to inspire me with respect, for I have made your books my own . . . and I unreservedly recognize the genuine authority of your criticism.

"As for data relative to myself, it is a privilege to give you anything you might think of interest. I am inexperienced in this matter, however, and you must pardon me if what I am sending proves unsuitable. But it seems to me that a bare outline of my experiences preceding any attempt—or, in truth, desire—to write might be interesting as revealing the background of real life behind my work, and as proving that I have not written out of the top of my head.

"I am thirty. My undergraduate college education was confined to a freshman year at Princeton University, class of 1910. My first job was secretary of a mail-order firm in New York. In 1909 I went with a mining engineer on a gold prospecting trip to Spanish Honduras, Central America. At the end of six months I was invalided home—tropical malarial fever—no gold. After that I became assistant manager of a theatrical company touring the East and Middle West. My first voyage to sea followed: sixty-five days on a Norwegian barque, Boston to Buenos Aires. In Argentine I worked at various occupations— in the draughting department of the Westinghouse Electrical Company, in the wool house of a packing plant at La Plata, in the office of the Singer Sewing Machine Company in Buenos Aires. Followed another voyage at sea, tending mules in a cattle steamer, Buenos Aires to Durban, (South) Africa, and return. After that a lengthy period of complete destitution in Buenos Aires—'on the beach'—terminated by my signing on as ordinary seaman on a British tramp steamer bound home for New York. My final experience at sea followed soon after this —able seaman on the American Line, New York-Southampton. The next winter I played a part in my father's vaudeville version of Monte Cristo, touring the Far West. Then I worked as reporter on the New London, Connecticut, *Telegraph*. My health broke down, my lungs being affected, and I spent six months in a sanatorium thinking it over. It was in this enforced period of reflection that the urge to write first came to me. The next fall—I was twenty-four—I began my first play —'The Web.' In 1914–1915 I was a student in Professor Baker's English 47 at Harvard. The summer of 1916 I spent at Provincetown. It was during that summer the Provincetown Players, who have made the original productions of nearly all my short plays in New York, were first organized. Is there anything in the above disconnected experiences which is of any service? I surely hope so."

A few days after this came, O'Neill wrote me another letter, saying, "I'm glad the stuff I sent you will fill the bill. I was rather afraid it looked as if I were making a Jack London hero of myself—whereas . . . I cannot recollect one heroic passage in those experiences!"

The outline is pretty accurate so far as it goes, but to begin at the beginning—

HE IS BORN

EUGENE GLADSTONE O'NEILL was born October 16, 1888, in a room on the third floor of the Barrett House, then an uptown family hotel on Broadway at 43rd Street, New York, for many years the Hotel Cadillac, and now replaced by a new building. He is the son of James O'Neill and Ella Quinlan, both of them devout Catholics. His father was one of the most gifted American romantic actors, a favorite from coast to coast, and his mother a quiet woman of whom we hear little, and whose influence over the boy can only be surmised. George Jean Nathan tells me that his own mother went to the same convent in Cleveland with Ella Quinlan, of whom she used to tell that the girl was strikingly beautiful and was looked up to by students and teachers alike as the most pious girl in the place. She was born in New Haven, and came to the Middle West in her early childhood. In marrying an actor she had had to give up family and friends. "My mother,"

O'Neill tells me, "was a fine pianist—exceptionally fine, I believe. I like good music, and always have, since my earliest childhood." James O'Neill was tall and handsome, one of the most impressive personalities in the theater of his generation. Booth had said of him that he could play Othello better than he could himself, and once O'Neill alternated with him. "My father," says the younger O'Neill, "was really a remarkable actor, but the enormous success of *Monte Cristo* kept him from doing other things. He could go out year after year and clear fifty thousand in a season. He believed at the time that he simply couldn't afford to do anything else. But in his later years he was full of bitter regrets. He felt that *Monte Cristo* had ruined his career as an artist."

To measure and appraise the influence of James O'Neill, Mrs. O'Neill, and their elder son on Eugene will be the task of some future biographer. They were a remarkable family. In his *Sixteen Authors to One* David Karsner speaks with evident authority of two persons who must have made a lasting impression on the boy Eugene. His brother Jim was a "waggish fellow, and when Eugene was old enough the brother began to teach him all that he knew of worldliness. This continued until Eugene was quite well into youthhood, but he soon learned to unlearn and discount his brother's tutelage." Jim, according to Tom Prideaux (who writes of O'Neill in *Life*, Oct. 14, 1946), knew most of the girls in show business, and when Eugene visited him in New York, "he took care that he was well entertained. 'The girls in those days,' says O'Neill, 'were less ambitious and more fun. While other boys were shivering themselves into a fit of embarrassment at the mere thought of a show girl, I really was a wise guy.'"

Then there was a Scotch nurse who, until the child turned seven, used to tell him horrible tales, and regale him with "sordid episodes, from the latest murder to the farthest terror that her whimsy could contrive." O'Neill told his interviewer, however, that the nurse was not unkind or cruel.

"My first seven years," writes O'Neill in a letter to Professor Arthur Hobson Quinn, who quotes it in his *History of the American Drama From the Civil War to the Present Day*, "were spent mainly in the larger towns all over the United States—my mother accompanying my father on his road tours in *Monte Cristo* and repertoire, although she was never an actress and had rather an aversion for the . . . stage in general." During the next six years he attended Catholic and non-sectarian boarding schools, and in 1902 was sent to Betts Academy at Stamford. "Usually," O'Neill told Fred Pasley, who reported the conversation in a series of articles in *The News* (New York, Jan. 1932), "a child has a regular, fixed home, but you might say I started in as a trouper. I knew only actors and the stage. My mother nursed me in the wings and in dressing rooms." The autumn after his graduation in 1906 he matriculated at Princeton, where he stayed until the following June. Before the final exams he was suspended for "general hell-raising"; specifically, it is said, for throwing a beer bottle through a window in President Wilson's house. Yet the incident could not have been too serious, and he might have returned, if he had wanted, somewhat later. But college did not appeal to him, so he took a job as secretary of a New York mail-order business in which his father had an interest. The firm sold "10-cent jewelry . . . giving an alleged phonograph with one record as a premium to children and seminary girls who disposed of the shabby baubles." His duties consisted mostly in attending to the correspondence, but I have been told that most of his work was done by a subordinate. O'Neill admits that he never took his job seriously, and when the firm went out of business he turned his back on the office with a sigh of relief.

In 1909 he married Kathleen Jenkins of New York, and the following year a son was born. Eugene Junior attended Yale and is said to have tried his hand at writing verse. He now teaches Greek at Yale. The married life of the young couple lasted only a short time. The marriage, characterized laconically as "a mistake," was formally ended by divorce in 1912.

Late in 1909 he set out on his gold-prospecting trip to Honduras. Though he is careful to minimize the importance and almost deny the presence of any romantic glamor in this and later exploits, there seems to be no doubt that he was impressed by the exotic scenes and people that formed the background of all his early years of wandering. Mr. Pasley (in the articles above mentioned) again quotes O'Neill on his Honduras venture: "It was my very first trip on my own. I expected to do a lot of jungle shooting. I wore a bandoleer slung from my right shoulder and carried a .30–.30 Winchester and a machete . . . all I ever bagged was a lizard."

O'Neill's favorite writers of fiction were Jack London, Conrad and Kipling; it was not until later that he read Marx, Kropotkin and Nietzsche. His first printed writings—as we shall see—were inspired largely by Kipling, London and Conrad.

When he returned home in 1910 his father was playing with Viola Allen in *The White Sister,* and Eugene was made assistant manager of the company. He toured with it from St. Louis to Boston for some months, was not especially interested in his job, and soon after the end of the season he set forth on his first sea voyage, a venture that was to have deep and lasting effects.

THE FIRST VOYAGE

THIS voyage of "sixty-five days on a Norwegian barque" took him to Buenos Aires. He worked there first for the Westinghouse Company, then for Swift at La Plata, and finally for the Singer Company in Buenos Aires again. These jobs were only stop-gaps, temporary and uncongenial occupations; he either walked out in disgust or was discharged in turn from each of them. "I landed in Buenos Aires," he said, "a gentleman so-called, and wound up a bum on the docks in fact." He liked to hang about the waterfront, making friends with sailors, stevedores, the down-and-outs. And he liked to drink. His bumming instincts, however pronounced, were not altogether vicious; he was not a hopeless failure. He had simply not found himself. Probably he was not yet even looking for himself. On the other hand, he was no literary chap in search of copy. He bunked with the outcasts because he was himself something of an outcast; he worked when he had to—when he could find a job—in order to pay for board, room and liquor, and on occasion for such crude forms of entertainment as he could find near the wharves or in the vicinity of Buenos Aires. He was "seeing life" with a vengeance.

In the evenings he used to go to the Sailor's Opera, "a large café to which all seamen automatically went. There the seaman yarned of adventures in strange seas, boasted of his exploits to officially pretty ladies, drank, played cards, fought and wallowed."

" 'It sure was a madhouse,' " said O'Neill to Louis Kalodyme in the latter's article, *O'Neill Lifts the Curtain on His Early Days,* published in the New York *Times,* Dec. 21, 1924, " 'but somehow a regular program was in progress. Everyone present was expected to contribute something. If your voice cracked your head usually did too. Some old sailor might get up and unroll a yarn, another might do a dance, or there would be a heated discussion between say Yankee and British sailors as to the respective prowess of their ships. And, if nothing else promised, a bit of a harmless fight could usually be depended upon as the inevitable star feature to round out the evening's entertainment.' "

So much of what he saw and heard and did has gone into the making of the early plays that some mention should also be made of the motion pictures at Barracas, a suburb of Buenos Aires.

" 'These moving pictures,' said O'Neill, 'were mighty rough stuff. Nothing was left to the imagination. Every form of perversity was enacted, and of course sailors flocked to them.

But, save for the usual exceptions, they were not vicious men. They were in the main honest, good-natured, unheroically courageous men trying to pass the time pleasantly.' "

Before long he went to sea again "tending mules on a cattle steamer, Buenos Aires to Durban, [South] Africa, and return." Having no cash, he was not allowed to remain there, or even to land. On his return to Buenos Aires there followed the "lengthy period of complete destitution . . . 'on the beach' —terminated by my signing as ordinary seaman on a British tramp steamer bound home for New York." This brings us to the year 1911.

JIMMY THE PRIEST'S

" 'IN NEW YORK,' he says, 'I lived at "Jimmy the Priest's," a waterfront dive, with a back room where you could sleep with your head on the table if you bought a schooner of beer.

" 'Jimmy the Priest's' was the original for 'Johnny the Priest's,' which is the saloon setting for the first act of *Anna Christie*. It was so named because 'Jimmy,' the proprietor, with his pale, thin, clean-shaven face, mild blue eyes and white hair seemed to be more suited for a cassock than the bartender's apron he wore. . . . ' "Jimmy the Priest's" certainly was a hell-hole. . . . It was awful. The house was almost coming down and the principal housewreckers were vermin. I was absolutely down, financially, those days, and you can get an idea of the kind of room I had when I tell you that the rent was three dollars a month. One roommate of mine jumped out of the window.' " (Quoted from Louis Kalodyme's article.) It will be seen, when I speak of *The Iceman Cometh*, that O'Neill was once more to make good use of the dive that served as the setting for the first act of *Anna Christie*.

"Again I hung around the waterfront for a while. There, as at Buenos Aires, I picked up an occasional job"—on a mail boat. After a few weeks, or months, "I shipped on the

American liner *New York,* as an able seaman. I made the
voyage to Southampton . . . and came back on the *Philadelphia.*"

One day, some time after his last voyage, he won at gam-
bling what was to him a large sum of money. Of course, that
meant a wild party. How long afterward he couldn't tell me,
but probably a day or two, when O'Neill regained consciousness, he found himself on a through train with a ticket for
New Orleans. Why New Orleans? No one knows.

BARNSTORMING

ON HIS arrival he learned that his father was playing the
ever-popular *Monte Cristo.* The prodigal presented himself to
his perplexed parent and appealed for money to buy a ticket
back to New York. The elder O'Neill was used to this kind
of appeal, and the boy's request was turned down. The story
is told that once Eugene and his elder brother Jim waited for
Monte Cristo at the stage door after a matinée performance.
Instead of asking point-blank for a gift they artfully reminded the actor of the big scene where he had slapped his
pockets and exultantly proclaimed that he had millions to
conquer the world with. Couldn't he loosen up and give them
a dollar?

I leave the story, because O'Neill admits it is characteristic
—but he tells me that it isn't true.

In New Orleans no fatted calf was served up and Eugene
was offered the choice of making his way back north by his
own devices or joining the troupe as an actor. New York is a
long way from New Orleans, so Eugene's name was added
to the payroll of the *Monte Cristo* company. He learned his
small part on the train and appeared for the first time as an
actor in Ogden, Utah. Charles Webster, who was in the company at the time, says that O'Neill played the unimportant
role of a jailer. Mr. Webster was amused by Eugene's apparent

astonishment at his—Webster's—ability to play three different parts in the same show. Sometimes when the elder O'Neill complained of his acting Eugene would gravely protest, declaring sarcastically it was a wonder that in such a show anyone could do anything at all, and do it decently. Mr. Prideaux' version of this is more pointed and dramatic. James is said to have told the youth, "Sir, I am not satisfied with your performance," and the youth had answered, "Sir, I am not satisfied with your play."

The company toured the Orpheum circuit in the Far West and at the close of the season, fifteen weeks later, the O'Neills returned to their summer home in New London.

HE BECOMES A REPORTER

THERE in August O'Neill began work as a cub reporter on the *Telegraph*. He did regular reporting and contributed verse to a "colyum" once or twice a week for nearly six months. It has been said that his half year as a newspaperman was a period of unhappiness and depression, but he assures me that he was usually happy, interested in his work, and fortunate in most of his personal associations. His friendship with the boss, Frederick P. Latimer, who liked and believed in him, meant a great deal in those days. "He's the first one," O'Neill says, "who really thought I had something to say, and believed I could say it."

"As we used to talk together," the Judge told me in 1925 when I went up to New London to see him, "and argue our different philosophies, I thought he was the most stubborn and irreconcilable social rebel I had ever met. We appreciated each other's sympathies, but to each, in the moralities and religious thought and political notions, the other was 'all wet.'

"He was the cub reporter," he went on, "and the four things about him that impressed me at once were his modesty, his native gentlemanliness, his wonderful eyes, and his literary style. It was evidence at once that this was no ordinary boy, and I watched what he thought, wrote and did with extreme interest. From flashes in the quality of the stuff he gave the paper, and the poems and play-manuscripts he showed me, I was so struck that I told his father Eugene did not have merely talent, but a very high order of genius. I believe I am the first who ever made that prediction. My notion at the time was that he would eventually abandon the poetic medium and become a novelist. While I've not been surprised at his success as a dramatist, I still cling to my original opinion."

But what was O'Neill like in the New London days, I wondered?

"His health was precarious," the Judge answered, "so much so that he had to quit work and betake himself to the out-of-doors, where I was often with him, especially on the water. He's always been fond of that. He was at one time in love with a very sweet young lady quite opposed to his radical ways of looking at things, and they were in the throes of breaking apart. He was adrift in mind and spirit, and the body was threatened. I was sorry for him, and sorry again because a good many of his local acquaintances were of a mildly Bohemian sort. . . . There was something in Eugene at that time—an innate nobility which inspires and drives a man against whatever hindrance to be himself, however Heaven or Hell conspires to rob him of that birthright.

"Emphatically he was 'different.' I thought it astonishing how keen was his wit, what a complete iconoclast he was, how richly he sympathized with the victims of man-made distress, how his imagination was running high as the festering skies above Ye Ancient Mariner; his descriptions strong and his spirit hot to produce something worth while for the sake of its own value and in utter scorn of its commercial value or conventional fame.

"I wouldn't," he concluded, "call Eugene a misanthrope by any means, even if he certainly is no Will Rogers. If he could only be in one of two places in a town—the church or the jail—I know where I would find him!"

The City Editor of *The Telegraph* was Malcolm Mollan, who set down a decade later some of his memories of the cub reporter (Philadelphia *Public Ledger,* Jan. 22, 1922): "I can see," he says, "the abashed, puzzled look of the boy as he carried away his beautifully written sketch. . . . 'This is a lovely story . . . but would you mind finding out the name of the gentleman who carved the lady and whether the dame is his wife or daughter or who? And phone the hospital for a hint as to whether she is dead or discharged or what? Then put the facts into a hundred and fifty words—and send this literary batik to the picture framers.' " But Mollan, like Latimer, was able to size up the young man and see in him something of what he might become. "The man," continues Mollan, "is as sensitive as a seismograph. There is no point of contact with human existence at which his finely spun nature does not detect and suffer from the discords and maladjustments of human affairs. It is quite impossible for his mind to dwell on a group of happily placed characters, for example, without reaching out further and discovering the inevitable underlying submerged group that has contributed to that happy placement!"

ILLNESS

IN DECEMBER, 1912, O'Neill's health broke down. Up to that time his existence had been, in a most literal sense, irregular: he had spent little time at home and for sixteen years he had been attending school, traveling with his parents, venturing forth on the high seas or drifting from job to job in North or South America; his nervous system, never too strong, had been seriously taxed by a good deal of hard and indiscriminate drinking. It had probably not occurred to him that it might be necessary to think of his health.

Now out of a clear sky the doctor told him he had a touch of tuberculosis, and for the first time he would have to take hold of himself. He was ordered to a sanatorium, and on Christmas Eve he entered Gaylord Farm at Wallingford, Connecticut. What he felt on entering the place may be understood by reading the opening pages of *The Straw*.

During the winter and spring of 1912–1913 he began, as he says, "thinking it over." At Gaylord the urge to write first came to him, the desire to express what he knew and felt about life.

He had dabbled in verse, and during his six months on the *Telegraph* he had learned something about putting "stories" into shape. But such writing as he had done was what nearly all young men turn out before they begin to grow up. Until the time of his breakdown he "never had any definite idea" as to what he wanted to do. "My father," he says, "was worried about me. He didn't know how to handle me, he didn't 'get' what I was trying to do; he only wanted me to settle down and make a living. He often used to think I was just crazy."

The five months at Gaylord marked a turning-point in his life. He says in the *Journal of Outdoor Life,* in 1923:

". . . It was at Gaylord that my mind got the chance to establish itself, to digest and evaluate the impressions of many past years in which one experience had crowded on another with never a second's reflection. At Gaylord I really thought about my life for the first time, about past and future. Undoubtedly the inactivity forced upon me by the life at a san forced me to mental activity, especially as I had always been high-strung and nervous temperamentally."

DISCHARGED AS ARRESTED

HE WAS "discharged as arrested," diagnosed as an uninteresting case, "there was so little wrong with him." In the late spring he spent some time with his family in New London, and when his father's season opened he went to live with the Rippins, an English family who had a home overlooking Long Island Sound. Here he stayed for more than a year, reading, resting, exercising—and writing. The doctor's warning had sunk deep, and he set to work building up his health. "I went swimming in the Sound," he told me, "every day during the winter."

On the authority of one member of the Rippin family who was present at the time, I should add that it was sometimes necessary to rout the young man out of a warm bed and make him hop into his bathing suit on pain of missing breakfast.

In fifteen or sixteen months' time he wrote eleven one-acters, two long plays, and some verse. The new life agreed with him. "After I left the san," he says, "I kept up the sleeping outdoors for over a year and kept pretty careful watch over myself generally. In fact, with more or less frequent lapses due to rehearsals in New York, etc., I've lived a pretty healthy outdoor life ever since. It's easy, for I much prefer it to city life anyway."

THE TURNING POINT

IT WOULD be hard to overestimate the importance of O'Neill's breakdown in the winter of 1912–13. The youth who entered Gaylord and the man who left it were two different beings. The first was occasionally a wild boy who loved life in the raw, whose restlessness and curiosity drove him away from family and friends in search of strange countries and still stranger men. He drank when he had the money, though that was not so very often. In the course of his wanderings he learned something about men, not their hypocritical manners and the masks they wear, but their minds and hearts, their ways of speaking and behaving. He was not an intruder in the underworld, but in some ways a part of it. Like Gorky he seems to have found in the lot of the outcast some consoling reality, some satisfactory reading of life.

Harry Kemp told me that once a feeble-minded boy of six formed a deep affection for O'Neill and O'Neill took pains to be kind. There was something strangely tender in the boy's longing to know things, and in the man's efforts to explain. One day the two were sitting on the wide yellow beach at Provincetown, looking out over the Atlantic. The boy wondered what was beyond Europe? "The horizon," answered O'Neill. "But what," persisted the lad, "is beyond the horizon?"

I don't mean to read a strange significance into the episode, but I think it not unreasonable to claim that in the unsocial misfits of our world the young O'Neill found something that he needed, something that was not to be found in normal ladies and gentlemen.

The drinking exploits of the early days were spectacular, and that surely accounts for the more spectacular tales that have been repeated about them. I have no wish to pass over nor minimize the importance of this matter, and O'Neill himself does not, of course, want to be whitewashed. But it stands to reason that no one could do as much work as he has done without the most rigid kind of self-discipline. He is continually solicitous about his health, for without that work is impossible, and work with him comes first. Physical exercise is a fetish. "I wanted," he tells me, "to be a two-fisted Jack London 'he-man' sailor, to knock 'em cold and eat 'em alive."

"At Provincetown," says Harry Kemp, "he used to lie on the beach for hours in his bathing-suit—when he was not working. He's one of the finest swimmers I've ever seen; he can do the Crawl as if he'd been born to it. He often used to go way out to the Point. Agnes [Mrs. O'Neill] was worried as hell, but nothing'd stop 'Gene. And you ought to have seen him in his Eskimo kayak! He'd get thinking out some idea, and round the Point in the roughest weather."

Plenty of exercise and hard work has been the rule since 1913. Kemp remembers how in the coldest days, at his old shack in Provincetown during the first year or two, O'Neill would wrap himself up in a blanket, put an oil-burner under him, and write for hour after hour. Though he was on friendly terms with other writers, he would hang the "Go to Hell" sign on his door when he was busy. He knew what he wanted, and he usually got it.

On leaving the sanatorium, he had made up his mind that he wanted to be a playwright. He had once thought he could write poetry: Judge Latimer told me Eugene didn't like it when he was told that his forte was prose, but O'Neill says that what he wrote for the paper was hardly ever serious verse. He was a reporter who contributed jingles to a "colyum"; that was part of his job. "You mustn't," he told me with a touch of impatience, "take seriously the stuff I wrote for the *Telegraph*. If I'd thought you were going to look up everything in the old files, I wouldn't have told you about it." But he has written a good deal in verse form that means something to him. He has a large notebook full of poetry, written at odd times over a fairly long period. He will not publish it, he says. Alfred Kreymborg told me that he saw several of the poems when he was editing *Broom*. The serious pieces "had fine stuff in them." But not quite what Kreymborg wanted.

The truth is that O'Neill was not cut out for a literary career in the conventional sense; he has never been a "literary" man. The pursuit of the *mot juste* has been of little importance to him compared with the search for life and the quest for an explanation of it. When he began work as a dramatist he was a young man with an insatiable zest for living and a limitless curiosity. He had begun to come to grips with existence, and the moment he had taken in all he could assimilate, he had to express it. The plays, of course, always came after, and grew out of his experience. He was, and always has been, a seeker of what lies beyond the horizon, of the elusive forms of beauty and truth that float in the imagination of the poet.

When he began writing in earnest his equipment was a clear mind, an innate sense of the theater, a sensitive and powerful imagination, and a fund of human experience—of a kind. He had read much, but not from a five-foot shelf; not for cultural purposes or self-improvement, but for spiritual sustenance. He was familiar with Nietzsche in translation before he went to Harvard, and there, with the help of a German grammar and dictionary, he read the whole of *Also Sprach Zarathustra* in the original. He wanted, too, a sufficient working knowledge of German to read the plays of Wedekind, few of which were then available in English.

By the time he was ready to write he knew a good deal about the show business, he had had some experience with his father's company, but what he knew of the old-school drama served mostly to intensify his dislike of its routine tricks.

His own earliest attempts show signs of revolt against the form and content of the American drama of the past; yet he knew something about that drama that convinced him that he wanted to make no use of its conventions. Besides, he was well up on recent drama. Even during his years of adventure and aimless wandering, he often went to the theater: as a son of James O'Neill he could get free seats at almost any box-office. He was especially impressed by Nazimova's first productions of Ibsen. He was also a voracious reader of plays, and during his stay at the Rippins' he read nearly all the time when he was not exercising or writing.

"I read about everything I could lay hands on: the Greeks, the Elizabethans—practically all the classics—and of course all the moderns. Ibsen and Strindberg, especially Strindberg."

HE GOES TO HARVARD

His year and more of 'prentice work had shown him that he needed some help on technical matters. What about Baker's "47" playwriting class at Harvard? Should he register for it?

It could do him no harm, certainly. So at the suggestion of his friend Clayton Hamilton, Eugene went to Cambridge in the fall of 1914. There he wrote two plays, *The Personal Equation*, in four acts (at one time called *The Second Engineer*), and a one-acter called *The Dear Doctor*.

A fellow-student records in a letter to me these impressions of the young O'Neill as a playwriting student in the classroom at Cambridge:

"My own memory of O'Neill is that he was good-looking, very nervous, extremely impatient with 47, and anxious to get down to live in Greenwich Village. I happen to remember two things he wrote: a one-act farce . . . which he called *The Dear Doctor*, and a long play about sea life called *The Second Engineer*. The first was inconspicuous (I don't know why the title sticks with me) and the latter was labored and stiff. His worst fault, I think, was an ineptitude at dialogue, except when the speakers were raving drunk, or profane. He was friendly, though rather uneasy and inarticulate at times. You got the impression that he trembled a little, and seemed trying to keep from stuttering. But when he delivered himself of a remark, it was impressive . . . I always thought him very likeable."

My correspondent adds that he was "foul-mouthed," but when I told this to O'Neill he smiled gleefully. "Foul-mouthed"—oh, no. The man who wrote the letter was a fastidious youth who looked as though he could be easily shocked, and that was why O'Neill would sometimes go out of his way to blaspheme after the fashion of sailors. He only did it to annoy!

Another classmate laconically states that the dark-eyed Irishman was a "sarcastic bastard."

A picturesque account of the Cambridge days was published some years ago by another classmate, John V. A. Weaver, under the title *I Knew Him When—*, in the New York *Sunday World* (February 26, 1926). Though Mr. Weaver waxes bitter at the end of his glowing story, and thinks 'Gene has become high-hat, what he writes is vivid and characteristic, if not exact in the details. Here are a couple of paragraphs:

"Going out of the class-room Elkins (the Society man) and myself moved on O'Neill. His diffidence seemed to have gone. We repaired to one of the Shamrock bars . . . We drank ale. We continued drinking ale until four in the morning, feet on the rail, one hand in the free lunch. It was just one of those nights. Ribald tales, anecdotes of experience, theorizing about the drama—what the collegians used to call a 'bull session.' A bull session de luxe. We piled finally into a decrepit hack. We fell into O'Neill's room some time about five. I had just purchased that day a copy of 'Spoon River Anthology.' When the dawn broke, I was sitting on a trunk, Elkins sprawled across the bed, O'Neill reading in his powerful, melancholy bass, poem after poem from that disturbing collection . . .

"Women were forever calling for 'Gene. There was something apparently irresistible in his strange combination of cruelty (around the mouth), intelligence (in his eyes), and sympathy (in his voice). I would not say that he was 'good-looking.' But one girl told me she could not get his face out of her thoughts. He was hard-boiled and whimsical. He was brutal and tender, so I was told. From shop girl to 'sassiety' queen, they all seemed to develop certain tendencies in his presence. What may have resulted, deponent sayeth not. About some things 'Gene was Sphinx-like. All I can report is the phenomena."

This article was quoted widely and the subject of it made no public comment, but it is only fair to say that O'Neill denies not so much the general spirit but the historical accuracy of the account.

What did O'Neill get out of his course in playwriting? I asked him one day.

"Well," he tells me, "not much out of the actual class-work itself. Necessarily, most of what Baker had to teach the beginners about the theater as a physical medium was old stuff to me. Though on one occasion Baker told me he didn't think *Bound East for Cardiff* (written before I entered the class) was a play at all, I respected his judgment. The plays I wrote for him were rotten. The long one was a rambling thing about a seamen's and firemen's strike. But it's funny about the one-acter. We thought it was slick enough for vaudeville, but when I began to look into the rights I found the story I'd based it on was stolen from a successful vaudeville sketch!— Yes, I did get a great deal from Baker—personally. He encouraged me, made me feel it was worth while going ahead. My personal association with him meant the devil of a lot to me at that time."

Professor Baker's own words, written in a letter to me (January, 1926) are worth quoting:

> "When O'Neill was working with me, he showed by the end of the year that he already knew how to write well in the one-act form, but he could not as yet manage the longer forms. I was very eager that he should return for a second year of work in these longer forms, but did not know till later that, though equally eager, his means at the moment made this impossible. O'Neill, when with me, worked steadily and with increasing effectiveness. He seemed absorbedly interested in what he was trying to do. Because of his wider experience of life, he seemed a good deal older than most of the men in the course, although not really so in years. He seemed a little aloof, though I never found him so personally. This, I think, came quite as much from a certain awe of him in his fellow-students because of his wider experiences, as from any holding apart by him . . . After all these years my pleasant memory of O'Neill in the work is far more vivid than the memory of the details of that work."

Not long after Baker's death, O'Neill contributed a few paragraphs to *George Pierce Baker, a Memorial* (1939). Among other things he wrote, "Not that the technical points, the analysis of the practice of playmaking taught in his class were not of inestimable value to us in learning our trade. But the most vital thing for us, as possible future artists and creators, to learn at that time (Good God! For anyone to learn anywhere at any time!) was to believe in our work and to keep on believing . . . He helped us to hope—and for that we owe him all the finest we have in memory of gratitude and friendship."

PROVINCETOWN

WHATEVER the reasons that ultimately shaped his course, O'Neill spent the winter of 1915–16 in and around Greenwich Village, New York, where he found congenial companions, mostly among the Radicals of the labor movement, I.W.W.'s, anarchists, and what he calls the "true native villagers," the Negro and Italian inhabitants of the quarter. It was not until he went to Provincetown that he came to know the people who founded the Players and were the pioneers in the movement: George Cram Cook, Susan Glaspell, Frank Shay, Frederick Burt, Mary Heaton Vorse, Wilbur Daniel Steele, Harry Kemp, E. J. Ballantine, Neith Boyce, and Hutchins Hapgood.

These young men and women, under the leadership of Cook, had played two short summer seasons of one-acters in 1915 and 1916. It was after the second summer that the Provincetown Players were formally organized, though as such they never played in the town that gave them their name.

The Wharf Theater, owned by Mary Heaton Vorse, was used for the production of four bills of one-acters and one review bill. This was in 1916, when O'Neill's first play was acted.

In *The Road to the Temple* Susan Glaspell tells how Margaret Steele had taken the old fish-house on the wharf for a studio, but she allowed Cook and his friends to use it, "so more people could come." Cook had dreamed of a theater where work done in the spirit of play should have "the only true seriousness." "Why not," he wondered, "write our own plays and put them on ourselves . . . ? A whole community working together, developing unsuspected talents." So the fish-house was made into a playhouse, and christened the Wharf Theater, with room for ninety people "if they didn't mind sitting close together on wooden benches with no backs."

"We gave a first bill," writes Miss Glaspell, "then met at our house to read plays for a second. Two Irishmen, one old and one young, had arrived and taken a shack up the street. 'Terry,' I said to the one not young, 'haven't you a play to read to us?'

" 'No,' said Terry Carlin, 'I don't write, I just think, and sometimes talk. But Mr. O'Neill has got a whole trunk full of plays,' he smiled.

"That didn't sound so promising, but I said: 'Well, tell Mr. O'Neill to come to our house at eight o'clock tonight, and bring some of his plays.'

"So 'Gene took *Bound East for Cardiff* from his trunk, and Freddie Burt read it to us, 'Gene staying out in the dining-room while the reading went on.

"He was not left alone in the dining-room when the reading had been finished.

"Then we knew what we were for."

Harry Kemp has given a fairly full account of the early days in Provincetown in "Out of Provincetown," *Theatre Magazine* (April, 1930). (Incidentally, he spells "Terry's" last name "Carline.") He relates that O'Neill had read one of his plays at a meeting held in Jack Reed's place, a play that was "frightfully bad, trite, and full of the most preposterous hokum. It was, as I remember, something about an American movie man who financed a Mexican revolution for the sake of filming its battles. One of the scenes depicted the hero's compelling the commanding generals on both sides—both being in his hire—to wage a battle all over again because it had not been fought the way he liked it!"

Everyone, it seemed, was restless in those days, ambitious, wanting to do something artistically important, and a playhouse was one means of using up the energy of young people who were all in their different ways conscious of a need for a new vision and a new power in the theater. George Cram Cook was the natural leader of such a venture.

"JIG" COOK

"Cook," O'Neill told me, "was the big man, the dominating and inspiring genius of the Players. Always enthusiastic, vital, impatient with everything that smacked of falsity or compromise, he represented the spirit of revolt against the old worn-out traditions, the commercial theater, the tawdry artificialities of the stage. I owe a tremendous lot to the Players —they encouraged me to write, and produced all my early and many of my later plays. But I can't honestly say I would not have gone on writing plays if it hadn't been for them. I had already gone too far ever to quit."

The question is not whether he would have gone on writing —there seems no doubt about that—but how far the Players helped him write the sort of plays he wrote. Miss Edna Kenton has given in the introductory pages of Cook's *Greek Coins* a careful statement of her opinion:

"But there is no doubt at all that had he not had our Playwrights' Theater and our experimental stage to use always precisely as he wished to use them, he would have reached Broadway by quite another road and with quite other plays . . . he had not only our stage; he had our 'subscription list,' and he used its members, bill after bill, season after season, in ways they could never dream of; played with them and never need for a thought of them except as stark laboratory reactions to his own experimentations. No other American playwright has ever had such prolonged preliminary freedom with stage and audience alike."

It is just as true that if it hadn't been for the plays of O'Neill and Miss Glaspell there would not have been much reason for the continuance of the Theater— and probably few subscribers.

At least at that time. But the Provincetown people had risen so often from their own ashes that they must now be acknowledged to have been the most ancient, honorable, and consistent of our aiders and abettors of young and unknown American playwrights.

If I had gone to Peakéd Hill in 1919 as I planned, I might now have described what the sleepy little fishing town looked like before it fell into the hands of hotel-keepers and their summer guests; but I first set eyes on the place one summer morning twelve years after the time I am now writing about. A wet fog hung over harbor and town, and the big feature of the main street was a gaudy movie-house called The Provincetown Theater. This monument to local enterprise stands only a couple of minutes' walk from the old Wharf Theater. The fog lifted, and for a moment the thin spit of shining sand they call the Point shot out across a wide expanse of smoking water. Outside the town everything looks about as it must always have looked, from the day the Pilgrims first set foot on shore beyond the Wharf to that afternoon when the gaunt young Irishman brought his trunkful of plays to Terry Carlin's shack. There are the desolate sand-dunes and the light blue sea, and the gnarled and stunted shrubs that fringe the marshes and rushy hollows.

Harry Kemp and Frank Shay have reminisced for my benefit in an effort to convey some notion of the days before O'Neill and the others had "arrived," when no one took himself too seriously. Out of Kemp's epic effusions ("They're great to listen to," O'Neill says, "even if the details aren't always right") I gather that the Tramp Poet wanted to buttonhole the playwright and get him to chin about books and poetry, but was never able to get very deep into a discussion. 'Gene would talk only about people or things that interested him, or else sit staring at nothing: he didn't have a damn word to say about literature. It was not for several years that Kemp gave up the hope of stretching out on one of the dunes and talking about Shelley to the accompaniment of the waves below. The dark Irishman remained stubbornly silent. Once, though, Kemp's hopes rose high when 'Gene, who liked to take long walks over from Peakéd Hill, got into the habit of stopping at the Kemps' house with some regularity. But again no long talks, because 'Gene, after silently retiring for a few moments, guessed he'd be going on again. Then Kemp tumbled, and the next time their visitor came he got no chance to retire, and was made to drink much more tea than he wanted. No talk, no bathroom, said Kemp to himself, till at last " 'Gene turned to me and confessed his back teeth were floating!" O'Neill has since admitted that the joke was on him.

Some day I hope Kemp will write out the whole story of the lonely writer O'Neill had invited to spend a few weeks with him during Mrs. O'Neill's absence. Both young men were in need of company. Kemp describes the man sitting for a couple of days face to face with his uncommunicative host, and at the end of a week rising up in rage and despair and cursing him before going home to enjoy his own company.

THE *THIRST* VOLUME

AMONG the plays O'Neill had brought with him to Provincetown were five that had already been published in book form. In 1914 Richard G. Badger of Boston issued in his American Dramatists' Series a thin book called *Thirst and Other One-act Plays by Eugene G. O'Neill*. The manuscript had been previously offered here and there, but no one would risk publishing it. Then Badger offered to do so on condition that the author should pay all the expenses. This the author couldn't do, so to James O'Neill, interpreter of the old romantic drama, we are indebted for guaranteeing the publication cost of the first plays of Eugene O'Neill, pioneer of a

new American drama. The book was not a success. Clayton
Hamilton says that he wrote the only review of it that ever
appeared. I have not seen his criticism, but I know what it
means to be encouraged by him. The notice of his young
friend's first book must have been kindly and encouraging.

O'Neill's father sent Eugene to Harvard with the hope that
he might find himself, and then he waited for something to
happen. It has been said that the old gentleman was hard on
the boy, objecting to Eugene's having anything to do with the
theater except, perhaps, as an actor; even that he kept him
penniless and practically a prisoner in the hope that poverty
might knock some practical sense into his head. Doubtless
he was worried; but, as O'Neill says, he was puzzled, perplexed and anxious. "He did believe in me—in a way, but
as I've said, he thought I was crazy. He didn't see why I
should write the kind of plays I did, and he pointed out,
quite properly, that there was no market for them; but he
must have thought there was something there—something he
did not like or maybe quite understand. He believed I might
some day amount to something—if I lived."

It is pleasant to know that the father was able to see his
boy's first work well received in the theater and, after the
manner of fathers, to pretend he "knew he had it in him all
the while." Someone said that he wept at a performance of
Beyond the Horizon.

In the *Times* article referred to above, it is related that
James O'Neill, greeting his son after the final curtain had
fallen, asked him if he was "trying to send the audience home
to commit suicide?"

FIRST PRODUCTION—*BOUND EAST FOR CARDIFF*

THE first O'Neill play ever produced, so far as I can learn,
was *Bound East for Cardiff*. It was done at the Wharf Theater
in Provincetown as the second bill of the summer season by

the group that was later to be known as the Provincetown Players. O'Neill acted the part of the Second Mate. I am told that his acting was not impressive, though it was not altogether bad.

Then came *Thirst*, in the fourth bill, and again O'Neill acted, this time as the Negro Sailor. Except for his appearance in a New York production of *Before Breakfast*, in which he undertook the role of the Arm of the non-speaking character, these are the only plays of his own in which he has acted.

That O'Neill was respected, listened to, and occasionally appreciated in those early days is clear from statements made by Frank Shay and others, and in the following passage written some years ago by Miss Kenton:

" 'You don't know 'Gene yet,' he [Cook] told me. 'You don't know his plays. But you will. And the world will know 'Gene's plays some day. This year, on the night he first came to Provincetown and read us *Bound East for Cardiff*, we knew we had something to go on with.' " Shay tells me that he and others who saw the first O'Neill productions immediately realized that the writer had something indescribably powerful in his make-up. "The effect produced on us by *Bound East* and *Thirst* was so strong we all felt instinctively we had had a profound experience."

Susan Glaspell, too, was just as deeply stirred. "I may see it through memories too emotional," she writes, "but it seems to me I have never sat before a more moving production than our *Bound East for Cardiff*. . . . Jig was Yank." The night of the opening there was a fog in the harbor, just as it is described in the script. "The tide was in, and it washed under us and around, spraying through the holes in the floor."

THE PROVINCETOWN PLAYERS

AFTER the summer season of 1916 the group returned to New York and, as the Provincetown Players, opened the Playwrights' Theater in Macdougal Street. That name was given it by O'Neill, and he insisted that only new American plays should be performed, although some of the group had wanted to experiment with Chekhov and other foreigners.

During the next four years all but one of his short plays were produced there. At first the Players took over a part of a brownstone-front house at 139 Macdougal Street, and, according to Pasley, "eight of the twenty-nine that had started in the old Provincetown fish-house had raised $30 each and the entire band of troubadours had fared boldly forth for New York City. The time was December of 1916. They had the parlor floor. The front was used for the auditorium—150 seats squeezed in by building them tier fashion. The rear room was the stage."

Two years later the little group moved to 133 Macdougal Street. Originally a dwelling, it had been used successively for various purposes, and it was a stable just before the Provincetowners moved in. Remodeled as a theater, it was used as long as the group operated, and is, even now, occasionally leased for tryout performances of a modest and tentative nature.

From the very first O'Neill had been trying his hand at long plays. He had worked hard after leaving the "san," at the Rippins' home, and at Cambridge under Professor Baker. He tells me that the stories describing him as a boor in the classroom are inventions. "I was one of the hardest-working students of the lot. But it's true that once someone started charting an Augustus Thomas play on the blackboard to show how it was built. I got up and left the room." At Provincetown Kemp says he never knew anyone who labored so consistently and so regularly. It was reasonable to hope that he might some day sell a manuscript to a Broadway manager. He not only hoped, he worked and planned.

THE *SMART SET* AND ITS EDITORS

MEANTIME there were other methods of making his way toward Broadway. Already in 1916 the venturesome Frank Shay had published in his *Provincetown Plays* O'Neill's *Before Breakfast* and *Bound East for Cardiff*. But there were wider horizons opening out. Like many of us who were growing up in those exciting years of the First World War, O'Neill used to read the criticisms of Mencken and Nathan in the *Smart Set* Magazine, and he had felt that these men offered a fresh and challenging point of view on art and literature. They also published one-act plays. Those laconic notes written on blue-gray paper must have kept many a writing youngster on his toes, and the checks, too, were a real help. The editors advised, on occasion, and they encouraged.

"The first [general] recognition of any kind that I received," says O'Neill, "was through The Smart Set. I sent three of my one-acters to Mencken, the editor. They were all three fo'c'sle plays, not at all the kind of thing The Smart Set prints. I wrote Mencken that I knew this, but that I merely wanted his opinion of them. I had a fine letter from him, saying that he liked them and was sending them to George Jean Nathan, the dramatic critic. I received a letter from Nathan also, and to my surprise the three plays were published in The Smart Set! . . ."

O'Neill says that this statement needs modification. For one thing, the Provincetown Players had already acted some of his plays, and *Seven Arts* Magazine printed not only his story *Tomorrow*, but accepted *In the Zone* for publication.

The printing of his plays in the *Smart Set* gave him a wider public than he had yet been able to reach, and recognition from Mencken and Nathan meant critical approval of a sort he had not to any great extent received.

In April, 1919, he wrote me: "My debt of gratitude to both Nathan and Mencken is great. From the first time they read two of my sea plays they have given me many a boost in spirit by their fair criticism and words of encouragement."

The three plays printed in the *Smart Set* were *The Long Voyage Home, 'Ile,* and *The Moon of the Caribbees.* They appeared in 1917 and 1918 It was later through the interest and enthusiasm of Nathan that *Beyond the Horizon* and *Gold* were brought to the attention of John D. Williams; it was Nathan, too, who was instrumental in selling *Anna Christie* and *The Fountain.*

TRYING TO SELL PLAYS

EVEN before O'Neill went to Harvard he had tried to place manuscripts through his own efforts. "I sent two of the plays," he says, "to a New York manager. After two years, having heard nothing from them, I wrote asking for their return." The same old story. George C. Tyler told O'Neill afterward that he had not read the scripts, "because plays by actors' sons are never any good!"

But if in the early days commercial managers returned his manuscripts, there were always the Provincetown Players and later the Greenwich Village Theater, ready to risk money and time and labor on any play he might offer.

LEADING DRAMATIST

SINCE the production of *Beyond the Horizon* in 1920 his position as our leading dramatist has not been seriously challenged, in spite of occasional attacks on him in which a certain amount of sound sense is often buried under indiscriminate abuse. The record from that time on is relatively brief and so far as external biographical data are concerned, of no great moment. Such facts as I think necessary for the proper understanding of his plays I shall mention in connection with my comments on the individual works. He has three times received the Pulitzer Prize, a medal for artistic achievement by the American Academy of Arts and Sciences, and in 1936 he received a Nobel Prize award. In 1926 he was given the degree of Doctor of Literature at Yale, as a "creative contributor of new and moving forms to one of the oldest of the arts, as the first American playwright to receive both wide and serious recognition upon the stage of Europe." As he stood before the assemblage of professors, trustees, scholars and mandarins at New Haven, he must have smiled to himself as he recalled the day when, sixteen years before, he had been fired from Princeton for "general hell-raising."

His fame has spread abroad: his plays are produced and read in nearly every country of the world. At the age of fifty-eight he has become an almost legendary figure.

Yet he is not known on the lecture platform, and few people would recognize him if they saw him on the street, which they probably would not have a chance to do. He rarely goes to the theater, though he is deeply interested in plays. In an interview in the New York *Herald Tribune* of Nov. 10, 1924, he said: "I hardly ever go to the theater . . . although I read all the plays I can get. I don't go to the theater because I can always do a better production in my mind. . . . Nor do I ever go to see one of my own plays—have seen only three of them since they started coming out. My real reason for this is that I was practically brought up in the theater . . . and I know [. . . too much about] the technique of acting . . . [Acting, except when rarely inspired, simply gets between me and the play] . . ." [1]

In 1946, in an interview reported in New York by Earl

---

[1] Here and later, I indicate the words or passages from published interviews which have been added to by O'Neill in my MS. or proofs. It was necessary to do this because O'Neill says that in nearly all the interviews there are errors. In a letter written to me in 1926, he states: "You have had enough experience to know how damnably inaccurate such interviews usually are. I can truthfully say that where I did not write out the stuff, what I have said has always been misrepresented. You could quote me to this effect . . . if you like."

Wilson, O'Neill commented: "By the time a dress rehearsal is over I'm sorry I ever wrote the thing and never do see it again—usually for about fifteen years. Some I haven't read for twenty years."

But he does attend, and with very few exceptions has always attended, his own rehearsals, and to a greater or less extent supervises the productions in all major matters. In the early days he would let Cook do most of the work, though he was not always in agreement with "Jig's" ideas.

He doesn't like to be interviewed, and as a rule he says very little when he is. The mass interview he gave to the press just before the opening of *The Iceman Cometh* in 1946, is an exception, and a notable one, to what I have just said. Unless he is among close friends, he seems rather "uneasy and inarticulate." When the late Benjamin de Casseres first met him several years ago, he tells us that he saw a "tragic, dignified, uncommunicative person; if he had said anything at all to me it probably would have been: 'Excuse me for not being nice, but I've just returned from hell.'" He is so seclusive that he will not eat in a restaurant if he can help it. He may conceivably like publicity and the ordinary varieties of adulation accorded to well-known men, but he has never shown any sign of it. He is a shy, retiring fellow who is mainly concerned with his thoughts and the plays that grow out of them; sensitive and somewhat nervous. Except where his work is concerned, he gives most people who meet him the impression that nothing else is of much consequence.

For two or three years he spent a good deal of his time at Brook Farm, his home near Ridgefield, Connecticut, with his wife and the two children of his second marriage. For a few summers since 1918 (with one exception) he lived at Peakéd Hill, a lonely reconditioned life-saving station near Provincetown. "I wish you could see my place up here," he wrote me in the summer of 1919. "It's an old U.S. life-saving station with not a house within three miles except the new station which is down the beach about half a mile away. If you get

up Cape way at all this summer be sure and come over to
'the Outside.' I'll promise the uniqueness of the place will repay you for the difficulty of getting here."

During the years 1925, 1926, and 1927, he spent several
months in a house at Paget East, Bermuda.

In 1918 he married Agnes Boulton. There were two children, a boy and a girl. Early in 1928 O'Neill went to Europe
and then to the Far East, where he stayed for several months.
During this period, and at various times thereafter, the
O'Neills did a great deal of traveling, in the Orient, in Europe, and in the United States. Late in 1928 he settled in a
chateau near Tours in France, and after his divorce, he married Carlotta Monterey. Mr. and Mrs. O'Neill returned to
America in the fall of 1931, spent the winter in New York
and then went to Sea Island, Georgia, where they built a
house, Casa Genotta. In 1936, after disposing of the house,
they went to the West Coast, and in Contra Costa County,
not far from Berkeley, they built another home, which they
called Tao House. There the O'Neills lived, with time out
occasionally for vacations, until 1944, when they moved to an
apartment hotel in San Francisco. Early in 1946 they came
back to New York, where they are (1947) apparently planning to settle down for a while.

Until recent years, when his working routine became seriously interrupted by long bouts of illness, O'Neill followed
a somewhat rigid daily schedule: he devoted nearly half his
day to writing and the rest of the time to swimming, boating,
tennis and other forms of exercise. If additional proof of his
"good" habits are required, I refer you to Mary B. Mullett's
article, "The Extraordinary Story of Eugene O'Neill," which
appeared in the *American Magazine* for November, 1922. The
writer set the seal of middle-class approval upon him when she
declared that he had a "regular habit of work."

From 1923 to 1927 he was associated with Kenneth Macgowan and Robert Edmond Jones in the management of the
Greenwich Village Theatre, and for a short period after the

reorganization of the Provincetown group he was one of its associate directors. What additional factual data on the man's life may be necessary will be found in the pages that follow, sometimes in separate sections and sometimes as parts of my analyses of the plays.

DRINKING

"Ask him what he used to drink," George Jean Nathan advised when I inquired how far he thought it tactful for me to go in discussing personal matters. "I know he used to take his whiskey straight, but in South America he must have had strange and wonderful concoctions. Remember, if he hadn't drunk the way he did and mixed with so many kinds of people in those early days we probably shouldn't have had his plays."

Not a bad idea, but I don't think the *kind* of drink makes so much difference. I see no falling off in our native literature since Prohibition was first tried, and conclude that the quality of a man's potations cannot seriously affect the quality of his writing. If it weren't that a part of the O'Neill legend centered round the question of drink I could dismiss it by saying that as a young man he drank heavily on occasion, while during the past twenty-odd years he has been, as he phrased it, "unfortunately" on the wagon. "Altogether too much damn nonsense," he told me when the matter first came up, "has been written since the beginning of time about the dissipation of artists. Why, there are fifty times more real drunkards among the Bohemians who only play at art, and probably more than that among the people who never think about art at all. The artist drinks, when he drinks at all, for relaxation, forgetfulness, excitement, for any purpose except his art. You've got to have all your critical and creative faculties about you when you're working. I never try to write a line when I'm not strictly on the wagon. I don't think anything worth reading was ever written by anyone who was drunk or even half-drunk when he wrote it. This is not morality, it's plain physiology. Dope I know nothing about, but I suspect that even De Quincey was boasting what a devil he was!"

Just when O'Neill began writing I am not sure, but it was probably in 1909, either before or during his first long trip. He wrote verse. It must have been crude and imitative, judging from the samples I have seen in the New London *Telegraph*, written three years afterward. These come next in order, for if he wrote anything else in his years of wandering, there is no record of it, and O'Neill doesn't remember.

Frederick P. (later Judge) Latimer, as I have already said, ran the New London *Telegraph* when O'Neill worked as a reporter for it. Besides his reporting the young man contributed light verse during the autumn and early winter of 1912.

A "COLYUM" POET

IN 1925 I went through the files of the *Telegraph* in the New London Public Library. O'Neill's contributions, except his reportorial write-ups, which I could not identify, are verses on the editorial page, most of them in a "colyum" under the heading *Laconics*. The first was printed August 26, and the last December 9. They are all signed, sometimes "E. O'Neill," sometimes "Eugene O'Neill," once "Tigean Te Oa'Neill," and once (to an ambitious political parody on *Hiawatha*) "Eugene Gladstone O'Neill." The twenty-four pieces show little beyond a youthful eagerness to play with verse-forms, though some have a touch of the earnestness which was to become one of his marked characteristics as a dramatist. Every one of them is a parody on some well-known poet or an imitation of some familiar poem. The chief influences I detected were Kipling and Villon, and the best parodies were on Walt Mason, Burns and Service. The year 1912 was teeming with political interest, and several of the longer verses were pointed topical satires. The following specimen, which I reprint in full, is typical. It appeared on September 28.

IT'S GREAT WHEN YOU GET IN

They told me the water was lovely,
    That I ought to go for a swim,
The air was maybe a trifle cool,
    "You won't mind it when you get in."

So I journeyed cheerfully beachward,
    And nobody put me wise,
But everyone boosted my courage
    With an earful of jovial lies.

The sound looked cold and clammy,
    The water seemed chilly and gray,
But I hastened into my bathing suit
    And floundered into the spray.

Believe me, the moment I touched it
    I realized then and there
That the fretful sea was not meant for me,
    But fixed for a polar bear.

I didn't swim for distance,
    I didn't do the crawl
(They asked why I failed to reach the raft,
    And I told them to hire a hall),

But I girded my icy garments
    Round my quaking limbs so blue,
And I beat it back to the bath house
    To warm up for an age or two.

I felt like a frozen mummy
    In an icy winding sheet.
It took me over an hour
    To calm my chattering teeth.

And I sympathized with Perry,
  I wept for Amundsen's woes,
As I tried to awaken some life in
  My still unconscious toes.

So be warned by my experience
  And shun the flowing sea,
When the chill winds of September
  Blow sad and drearily.

Heed not the tempter's chatter,
  Pass them the skeptic's grin,
For the greatest bull that a boob can pull
  Is "It's great when you get in."
                              —E. G. O'Neill.

Perhaps it was not altogether chance that caused him to hand in as his farewell contribution a parody on *Blow, Blow, Thou Winter Wind*, the refrain of which expresses a loathing for December weather.

As I looked through the other "poems" I found a great deal that is callow, and precious few signs of any literary gift. Yet there was a line here and there that brought me to a sudden stop. The following quatrain might stand appropriately on the title-page of *The Moon of the Caribbees*:

For it's grand to lie on the hatches
  In the glowing tropic night,
When the sky is clear and the stars seem near
  And the wake is a trail of light.

Only a few verses were written at the sanatorium; by that time O'Neill had begun seriously thinking about the theater. His contributions to the *Telegraph* were his artistic wild oats, and I have referred to them only because they are a part of his development as a writer. At O'Neill's request I have omitted a few other samples transcribed from the *Telegraph*. "You're reading meanings into my stuff," he told me. "I was trying to write popular humorous journalistic verse for a small-town paper, and the stuff should be judged—nearly all of it—by that intent."

In 1930 Ralph Sanborn, enthusiastic collector of O'Neilliana and an irrepressibly conscientious investigator, tracked down all the O'Neill printed verse that he could identify. When he proposed to me that we prepare a bibliography of O'Neill's works,[1] I agreed, and the book was published in 1931, Sanborn having done nearly all the work. Not satisfied with listing the plays, he proceeded to lift all the verse that had appeared in the *Telegraph* and print that, together with the fugitive verse that he discovered elsewhere. He found that the first sample of our author's printed work was a poem called *Free*. This was privately published in April of 1912, in the *Pleiades Club Year Book*. Other verse was contributed in 1914, 1915 and 1917, respectively, to the New York *Call*, "The Conning Tower" column of the New York *Tribune,* and *The Masses.*

---

[1] *A Bibliography of the Works of Eugene O'Neill,* by Ralph Sanborn and Barrett H. Clark. Random House, New York, 1931.

THE PLAYS

THE PLATES

THE EARLIEST PLAYS

OF THE thirteen plays he wrote before going to Cambridge, only six have survived. The earliest, never produced or published, was *A Wife for Life*. It was written for the vaudeville stage. The idea for it had come to him when he was playing the Orpheum circuit with his father, and the writing was done shortly after he left Gaylord. He told me it was the first and last play he ever wrote with an eye on the box-office. He adds that it was the worst thing he ever did.

The first of his plays that was preserved is *The Web*. It was written early in the fall of 1913, and printed in the *Thirst* volume the next year.

THIRST AND OTHER PLAYS

OF THE one-acters written in 1914, only *Thirst, Recklessness, Warnings,* and *Bound East for Cardiff* were kept. A long play, *Bread and Butter*, and a short one, *Abortion*, were destroyed—and neither was ever acted. *Thirst* and *Bound East* were produced by the Provincetown Players two years later.

This brings us to the first group of plays on which we can form any judgment, *Thirst,* and the four others in the volume with it.

The five pieces in the *Thirst* volume are now definitely repudiated, and will never be reprinted with O'Neill's permission. Only two have had authorized productions—*Thirst* and *Fog,* though all of them have been acted by amateurs.

The Web comes first in order of composition. It will give satisfaction to those who once complained of O'Neill's profanity to know that the earliest of his surviving plays opens with "Gawd! What a night!" This is a crude melodramatic piece about a prostitute and her protector. The scene is a "squalid bedroom on the top floor of a rooming house on the lower East Side, New York." The woman has a baby, which annoys Steve, and when he knocks her down another man comes to the rescue in the nick of time. The bully tells her that if she leaves or "holds out" on him he will send her to jail and take the child away from her. Caught in the web! The newcomer, a fugitive from justice, is attracted by the woman and gives her money to go away with; but Steve, who has been hiding nearby, re-enters, kills the other man and "plants" the revolver in order to implicate the woman when the police arrive, which they don't fail to do the very next moment. The woman is taken away, while the baby cries "Maamaaaa." One of the plainclothes men takes the infant and speaks to it: "Mama's gone now. I'm your mama now." Curtain.

Thirst, called a "tragedy," is more original in conception. There are just three characters: a gentleman, a dancer, and a West Indian mulatto sailor, and the scene passes on the life raft of a wrecked steamer in mid-ocean. "Here and there on the still surface of the sea, the fins of sharks may be seen slowly cutting the surface of the water in lazy circles." The play opens with these lines:

> THE DANCER—(*Raising herself to a sitting posture and turning piteously to the Gentleman.*) "My God! My God! This silence is driving me mad! Why do you not speak to me? Is there no ship in sight yet?"

The episode shows three sorry remnants of humanity dying of thirst. The sailor sits apart crooning a "monotonous Negro song." The gentleman and the dancer are convinced that he has a supply of drinking water hidden somewhere, and the woman approaches him and offers her necklace for a drink, but the sailor persists in denying that he has water. The woman then offers herself, but the stolid Negro is unmoved.

When, shortly after, she dies, the Negro begins to show an interest in life, sharpens his knife and, glancing toward the body, addresses the gentleman: "We shall eat. We shall drink," whereupon the gentleman pushes the woman's body into the sea. The Negro, mad with rage, plunges his knife into the other's back, is himself caught in the desperate embrace of the wounded man, and the two totter off the edge of the raft. "The sun glares down like a great angry eye of God. . . . On the raft the diamond necklace lies glittering in the blazing sunshine."

The play is written in an exaggerated, violent and rhetorical style, but there is undeniably an air of sincerity about it. The basic idea is reminiscent of Jack London and I would not be surprised to learn that the development of the situation owes something to the vivid scenes in the closing chapters of *The Call of the Wild*.

The best that can be said of *Thirst* is that it is a forthright and daring melodramatic scene.

Recklessness is a swift-moving drama of revenge, as conventional as any Grand Guignol thriller. A husband returns home and learns that his wife is having an affair with the chauffeur; after getting the facts from a jealous maid, he sends the chauffeur out, knowing that the steering-gear of the car is out of order—and we are left to shudder at the knowledge that he rides to certain death.—He does, and when his body is brought in, the woman kills herself.

Warnings is in two scenes. The first shows us a wireless operator in his home: a typical slice of life from the bread-and-butter Bronx type of realistic play popularized by Eugene Walter. Knapp works aboard a transatlantic liner, and has just learned that he may become stone-deaf at any moment; but for the sake of his family he doesn't dare report the facts to his employers.

The second scene is in Knapp's cabin aboard ship in mid-ocean. The steamer is sinking and the operator is desperately signaling for help, but he can get no answer.

"Oh, my God! It's come!" he cries to the Captain. "I can't hear anything. It's happened just as the doctor said it might. . . . Oh, I should have told you, sir, before we started—but we're so poor, and I . . ." etc. He then shoots himself.

There is the germ of a good play here—or, perhaps, of a good scene only—but the young dramatist worked out his idea too literally, without the necessary skill or imagination. To begin with, it was hardly necessary to write a whole scene showing the man's family: all the playwright had to do was to make it clear that the operator could not afford to give up his job. Then—a more serious matter—there was no need for Knapp to blurt out what the doctor had told him. If he had suddenly and without warning gone deaf, he could hardly have been blamed for that, and since he was prepared to lie about the matter he might easily have planned an acceptable lie. Of course, the point is that he feels his responsibility, but it might take some time for his conscience to drive him to a confession of guilt.

Fog, the best piece in the book, is the earliest of the O'Neill plays to show the writer's attempt to reach out beyond the limits of literal surface realism, the first to carry out successfully the particular kind of "super-naturalism" he was later to use with notable effect.

The scene is the "life-boat of a passenger-steamer drifting helplessly off the Grand Banks of Newfoundland. A dense fog lies heavily upon the still sea." The characters are a Poet, a Man of Business, a Polish Peasant Woman, a Dead Child, Sailors, and an Officer. Together in the boat are the Poet, the Business Man, the Woman and her Dead Child. They drift up to the edge of an iceberg, where they wait for help. They hear a steamer whistle, but the Poet, to save the steamer from running into the iceberg, prevents the Business Man from calling. We see by this time that the play is not conceived as a realistic transcript from life: the Poet is a symbolic embodiment of idealism, and the Business Man an abstract figure suggesting materialism. For the moment it looks as though all were lost;

then the fog lifts and the boat approaches. The Sailors have been guided to them by the voice of the Child. Meantime the Peasant Woman has died. The scene is quite dramatic:

> THE OFFICER—Too bad! But the child is all right, of course?
> THE POET—The child has been dead twenty-four hours. He died at dawn yesterday . . .

Fog is a parable with a sudden flash of beauty at the end. Technically it foreshadows the so-called Expressionistic scenes in *The Hairy Ape.*

What one would think of the five plays in *Thirst* if one knew nothing else of their author's work is now hard to say. It is easy to see in them an occasional indication of talent, to read into them signs of promise—if you happen to read the book after seeing its author's later work. But I cannot see in them anything more than experiments by a somewhat talented beginner. They show some knowledge of the technical side of play-building, and they are potentially dramatic. Best of all, they show the young man trying to tell something about life. Except in *Warnings,* he has gone to the heart of his situation and tried to dramatize it; but in characterization and dialogue he is noticeably deficient. Here he follows conventional fiction and melodrama; he is not yet able to make use to any great extent of what he knows of life and he is, naturally enough for a beginner, too eager to introduce into his plots ready-made violence in the form of murder and suicide.

EXPERIMENT

His next two plays were full-length: *Bread and Butter*—in four acts, and *Servitude*—in three. Neither was ever acted or printed, and in the official list they are marked "destroyed." Both were written in 1914, before O'Neill went to Harvard.

Bound East for Cardiff, the one really mature play he wrote

in the 'prentice years, belongs to the year 1914. He says
(1935) it was written at New London, spring of 1914, "during my first year of play-writing." It was followed by *Abortion*, another one-acter, produced in 1916 but never printed.
In 1915 came the two plays written under Baker in English
47, the one-act adaptation called *The Dear Doctor*, and the
long play, *The Second Engineer*, also called *The Personal
Equation*, which have already been mentioned. To 1915 also
belong the one-acters, *A Knock at the Door* (a comedy), *The
Sniper*, and *Belshazzar*, a Biblical play in six scenes, written in
collaboration with a friend and fellow-student, Colin Ford.
The first and last were never acted or printed, but *The Sniper*
was produced by the Provincetown Players in New York in
1917. It has not been published.

I read a script of *The Sniper* when I was going through the
files at the office of The Provincetown Playhouse, perhaps the
only one in existence. It is far better than most of the plays in
Thirst. It tells of a Belgian peasant whose son and wife have
been killed by German soldiers. In desperation he defies orders
and begins shooting Prussian soldiers as they march through
his village. He is soon captured and shot. Sentimental though
much of the writing is, *The Sniper* is none the less an exciting
little scene.

Eight short plays and one long one were written in 1916.
Four of these were destroyed without having been printed or
acted: *The Movie Man*, a comedy; *Atrocity*, a pantomime;
The G.A.M., a farce-comedy, and *Now I Ask You*, a farce-
comedy in three acts.

The plays that were kept are *Before Breakfast*, *'Ile*, *In the
Zone*, *The Long Voyage Home*, and *The Moon of the Caribbees*.

In 1917 no plays were written,[1] only the short story *To-*

---

[1] This statement is based on a supposedly authentic list published in the late
twenties. In the Wilderness Edition (1935), O'Neill has, however, affixed short
notes to each volume, telling when and where each of the plays printed there
was written. There is some discrepancy between the list I have used and O'Neill's
own notes, but the matter is not very important anyway.

morrow, which was printed in *Seven Arts* Magazine. It is based on an episode in the life of an Englishman O'Neill had lived with in New York. He had been a war correspondent and had later suffered misfortune in many forms. "When I knew him he always lived in the land of tomorrow. When he'd get a job on a newspaper he'd last a few days and then get dead drunk on the first week's pay." The story is not particularly remarkable, but is worth noting that in *The Iceman Cometh* the Englishman has been transformed into the character of Jimmy Tomorrow. In 1918 he wrote the first of his long plays that reached the stage, *Beyond the Horizon.* Only two of that year's plays were not produced: *Till We Meet* and *Shell-shock,* both in one act. *The Rope, The Dreamy Kid,* and *Where the Cross Is Made*—all one-acts—were produced and published. A long play—*The Straw,* acted in 1921 —was written toward the end of the year.

Then in 1919 came three one-act plays: *Honor Among the Bradleys, The Trumpet,* and *Exorcism.* Only *Exorcism* was produced, and none have been printed. *Exorcism* tells of a young man who finds life hard to bear in the slums where he is forced to exist. He takes poison, but two drunken friends call a doctor, who arrives just in time to save him.

The long play, *Chris Christopherson,* was also written in 1919.

From this time onward he wrote no more one-act plays until the early 1940's.

With the production of *Beyond the Horizon* early in 1920, O'Neill's period of trial and apprenticeship had come to a close.

"I am no longer interested," he said in the New York *Herald Tribune* (Nov. 16, 1924), "in the one-act play. It is an unsatisfactory form—cannot go far enough. The one-act play, however, is a fine vehicle for something poetical, for something spiritual in feeling that cannot be carried through a long play."

THE MOON OF THE CARIBBEES AND
OTHER ONE-ACTERS

EARLY in 1919 *The Moon of the Caribbees and Six Other Plays of the Sea* was published in book form. Besides the title play the volume included *Bound East for Cardiff*, *The Long Voyage Home*, *In the Zone*, *'Ile*, *Where the Cross Is Made*, and *The Rope*.

The first of these I ever saw produced was *In the Zone*. The impression of that production was still fresh in my mind when in May, 1919, I opened the new volume. I was reviewing books for the New York *Sun* at the time, and I told Grant Overton, the book editor, that I thought this O'Neill man deserved a special article. "Go ahead," he assented. "I've heard fine things about the young fellow. Take all the space you need."

My article ended with the words:

"Having demonstrated his skill in the one-act form and, at least to me and his manager, in the three-act, I see no reason why O'Neill should fail to be recognized as our leading dramatist. O'Neill is not perfect, he is not free from defects of characterization and style, but he is better equipped than any other young American. He promised five years ago, with his *Thirst* and other plays; since then he has fulfilled his promise; he has now only to develop, to widen his vision of men and women and do his best, unhampered by the material success that is sure to come to him."

In this article I had given high praise to *In the Zone*, but my remarks called forth an interesting letter from O'Neill, in which he said:

". . . I by no means agree with you in your high estimate of *In the Zone*. To me it seems the least significant of all the plays. It is too facile in its conventional technique, too full of clever theatrical tricks, and its long run as a successful headliner in vaudeville proves conclusively to my mind that there must be 'something rotten in Denmark.' At any rate, this play in no way represents the true me or what I desire to express. It is a situation drama lacking in all spiritual import—there is no big feeling for life inspiring it. Given the plot and a moderate ability to characterize, any industrious playwright could have reeled it off . . . I consider *In the Zone* a conventional construction of the theater as it is."

I still feel that O'Neill was expressing here his impatience over popular approval. *In the Zone* had made a hit; how, therefore, could it be really first class? It is an episode that unfolds aboard the tramp steamer *Glencairn*. The year is 1915, and the time midnight, just after the ship has entered the submarine zone. In the fo'c'sle the sailors are in a state of high nervous tension. One of them, Smitty, behaves suspiciously, and this leads the others to believe he is a German spy. They start to take a box from his trunk which they fear may be filled with explosives. They cautiously dump it into a pail of water and open it. Smitty comes in quietly and discovers what his shipmates are about, but before he can do anything they seize him and tie him to his bunk. In the box they discover only a bundle of letters from the girl Smitty had been engaged to, and in reading them they learn what has happened: she had thrown him over because he drank, and he had gone to sea in desperation. As the story unfolds, the men are ashamed, and at the end they release Smitty in silence. From one of the letters a dried flower flutters and falls to the floor. How O'Neill must regret that touch!

But for all its conventionality, *In the Zone* belongs in the O'Neill canon just as logically as the far better *Moon of the Caribbees*. It belongs because sentiment of a rather obvious sort, and soft-heartedness and pity and romance, are fundamental parts of the characters of Smitty and Cocky and nearly all the other members of the group who play leading roles in his four one-acters, which were later produced under the general title of *S.S. Glencairn*. *In the Zone* is a bit of sentimental drama, smooth and theatrically effective; it is a necessary part of the entire cycle of related sea plays.

THE BACKGROUND OF THE SEA PLAYS

THE curious thing about *In the Zone* is that without the three others in the series it is not so true to life nor so effective; and it is no less curious that *The Moon of the Caribbees, Bound East* and *The Long Voyage Home*, without *In the Zone*, seem incomplete, and not so true nor so effective either as drama or as a picture of fo'c'sle life.

No, O'Neill wrought better than he knew when he wrote *In the Zone*. And I found on seeing the *Glencairn* group acted again that O'Neill brought into each of the plays a note of sentiment to finish off the picture. In *Bound East* Driscoll is "sayin' 'is prayers"; and in *The Long Voyage Home* a pathetic sailor is done in by landlubbers. The play closes with a touch of irony to conceal the underlying pathos, while in *The Moon of the Caribbees* we have Smitty tenderly reminiscing.

Yet, all things considered, *The Moon of the Caribbees* is no doubt a finer piece of work than *In the Zone*. In the letter quoted above O'Neill continues:

O'NEILL ON THE SEA PLAYS

". . . Whereas, *The Moon of the Caribbees*, for example— (my favorite)—is distinctively my own. The spirit of the sea —a big thing—is in this latter play the hero. While *In the Zone* might have happened just as well, if less picturesquely, in a boarding house of munition workers. Let me illustrate by a concrete example what I am trying to get at. Smitty in the stuffy, grease-paint atmosphere of *In the Zone* is magnified into a hero who attracts our sentimental sympathy. In *The Moon*, posed against a background of that beauty, sad because it is eternal, which is one of the revealing moods of the sea's truth, his silhouetted gestures of self-pity are reduced to their proper insignificance, his thin whine of weakness is lost in the silence which it was mean enough to disturb, we get the perspective to judge him—and the others—and we find his sentimental posing much more out of harmony with truth, much less in tune with beauty, than the honest vulgarity of his mates. To me *The Moon* works with truth, and *Beyond the Horizon* also, while *In the Zone* substitutes theatrical sentimentalism. I will say nothing of the worth of the method used in the two short plays save that I consider *In the Zone* a conventional construction of the theater as it is, and *The Moon* an attempt to achieve a higher plane of bigger, finer values. But I hope to have all this out with you when we meet. Perhaps I can explain the nature of my feeling for the impelling, inscrutable forces behind life which it is my ambition to at least faintly shadow at their work in my plays."

I did not see *The Moon* until it was revived a year or two after it came out in book form, or I might have been more enthusiastic in my early review of it. I see in it a fairly successful attempt to suggest certain sensations through the use of rhythmical prose—not alone the spirit of the sea, but of man's loneliness in the presence of nature. O'Neill has indeed created, with the meagerest effects, a background for his drama, setting against it one poor relic of broken manhood.

But something is lacking, and the play is not so complete a revelation of the dramatist's mood as he considered it. O'Neill has conceived his situation and characters as a short, sharp episode in a vast epic, which is only faintly suggested. The words uttered by his men and women, true and fitting as they are, somehow fail to set vibrating within me the chords that he must have heard when his idea first came to him. They are somewhat thin, they lack that richness that lends to Conrad's words (I mean his dialogue—it is not fair to compare his descriptions to the dialogue of a dramatist) the full magic of poetry. O'Neill leaves too much to the director and the stage-carpenter: for drama which is poetic in conception should be poetic in execution. But *The Moon of the Caribbees* is none the less a play of considerable power. There is practically no story in it: a sailor speaks aloud his dreams and disappointments, while his mates carouse. There is a fight, a man is killed, and the curtain falls.

No wonder O'Neill looks upon this play with paternal fondness. It was, as he says, his "first real break with theatrical traditions. Once I had taken this initial step, other plays followed logically."

I have already spoken of *Bound East for Cardiff*. Of the score of plays written during the first three years, this is easily the best. It was the first of the O'Neill plays to be produced. The scene, like that of *In the Zone*, is laid in the fo'c'sle of the S.S. *Glencairn*, and the principal characters are the same as those in *The Long Voyage Home* and *The Moon*. The incident occurs during a "foggy night midway on the voyage between New York and Cardiff." The sailor Yank lies dying in his bunk while the others tell yarns and swap reminiscences. Yank takes a turn for the worse, quietly rambles on, wishing he had never gone to sea, and dies. An unpretentious episode, moving and tense, yet with hardly a vestige of "theater" in the conventional sense of the word. It is hard to believe that *Recklessness* and *Warnings* were written by the same man in the same year.

The Long Voyage Home is more elaborate; it is, as George Middleton said of his own one-act plays, the "epitome of a larger drama which is suggested in the background." Middleton had taken the short play very seriously.

The scene is the bar of a "low dive on the London waterfront." The crew of the *Glencairn* have just been paid off. Olson the Swede, with two years' savings in his pocket, wisely refuses to drink. He has been planning for a long time to go home and settle on a farm, but every time he had got his pay he squandered it. At last it looks as though he were about to realize his dream. But he is tricked by a scheming couple into taking a soft drink—which is drugged. They rob him, carry him out, and put him aboard a ship bound on a two years' voyage round the Horn.

His comrades come back and find him gone. They are told he has disappeared with one of the girls, and Driscoll grins: "Who'd think Ollie'd be such a divil wid the wimmin? 'Tis lucky he's sober or she'd have him stripped to his last ha'penny. (*Turning to* COCKY, *who is blinking sleepily.*) What'll ye have, ye little scut? (*To* JOE) Give me whiskey. Irish whiskey!"

That is all. The ironic note at the end is characteristic. While there is something pathetic and painful about the incident, it is hardly tragic. The Swede's ill fortune is brought about by a trick: the fellow's predicament is scarcely more than a case of hard luck.

In *'Ile* we have something far different. The theme is one that Balzac never tired of using—the consuming passion of a man to accomplish a set purpose. Captain Keeny is a hard New England whaling captain dominated by an unconquerable pride. At the end of the two years' period his crew have signed up for he has only a small part of his quota of whale "ile." "It ain't the damned money," he says, "what's keepin' me up in the Northern Seas, Tom, but I can't go back to Homeport with a measly four hundred barrel of ile. I'd die fust. I ain't never come back home in all my days without a full ship. Ain't that the truth?" The crew are mutinous, and the Captain's wife is almost out of her head from loneliness and anxiety. Only the prospect of her complete breakdown alters his determination to push on for the "ile," and seeing her condition he agrees to sail for home; but the instant open water is ahead and whales are sighted, he changes his mind. Mrs. Keeny, her mind evidently on the point of collapse, no longer knows what is happening.

Here is the stuff of tragedy, and *'Ile* is about as near to tragedy as any one-act play can come. We sense here no "fixed" situation contrived to produce a theatrical "kick." A man is driven by an irresistible passion; opposed to him are a mutinous crew, and a wife whose happiness, sanity, life, perhaps, depend on his returning home. Here are the elements that precipitate the tragedy. In the moment of his trial the man's character is tested to the limit; and because of what he is, he makes his momentous decision.

The Moon of the Caribbees, for all the richness of its atmosphere, cannot compare with *'Ile*. In *'Ile* I feel the inevitability of the tragic ending: it seems almost as though the dramatist were holding back the ultimate truth that lies at the heart of his situation, hesitating to state it in all its bald cruelty.

It is only the second-rater who makes you feel that he rather enjoys the sorrow and terror of the figures he has created. Perhaps that is why the work of the great tragic poets is always tempered with compassion, and why O'Neill himself in certain of his later plays, seemingly impatient with the accidental, or incidental, elements in man's character that too often precipitate tragic conflict and defeat, has dehumanized his dramatis personae and permitted himself to drive them to extraordinary deeds of violence, without our feeling that his victims are too close to us, too much like the common run of men.

The next play in the volume is a by-product. In a letter to George Jean Nathan, O'Neill says of it:

"I suppose I shall be credited on all sides with having made *Where the Cross Is Made* into a long play, yet the reverse is the real truth. The idea of *Gold* was a long play from its inception. I merely took the last act situation and jammed it into the one-act form because I wanted to be represented on the Province-town Players' opening bill two seasons ago. I mention this only because I know how impossible it is to expand a natural short play into a long one, and would hardly make such a futile mistake. *Gold* was always full length to me."

The play is crude and obvious melodrama. The plot requires far too much explanation, and even when that is made and we are ready to watch the events we have been prepared for, what remains is at best little more than a theatrical stunt. In another letter to Nathan he says: ". . . But where did you get the idea that I really valued *Where the Cross Is Made?* It was great fun to write, theatrically very thrilling, an amusing experiment in treating the audience as insane—that is all it means or ever meant to me. . . ."

Since the piece is a part of the long play *Gold,* there is no use saying any more about it here.

The Rope is the last play in *The Moon of the Caribbees* collection. It was the bitterest and in some respects the most mature play he had written up to the year 1918. It is a study in hatred. The central character is Abraham Bentley, a miser, a hard, militant-Christian New Englander, like Ephraim in *Desire Under the Elms.*

The Rope shows us an ugly set of characters, some of them bordering on the grotesque; though it is overladen with talk about the past history of the people, it has an occasional grim beauty in it. "There is," as O'Neill said a few years later, "beauty even in its [life's] ugliness." There is rarely any beauty that does not have its roots in what is, or at first seems to be, ugliness. It is the artist's affair to discover, feel and at last reveal the beauty that underlies everything in the world.

The Rope is the first of a kind of play that O'Neill in after years was to develop into a powerful and effective art-form. *Diff'rent* stems from it, and *Desire Under the Elms,* and *The Iceman Cometh,* all of them, in parts, lyric emanations from the back-wash of life, hymns to the vitality of man. O'Neill was as yet unable to handle his materials with the ease of a mature craftsman, but he must have had intimations of the goal he was aiming at.

BEFORE BREAKFAST AND THE DREAMY KID

THERE are two other one-act plays (not in *The Moon of the Caribbees* volume) that should be mentioned here: *Before Breakfast* and *The Dreamy Kid.*

Before Breakfast, written at Provincetown in the summer of 1916, is a technical stunt not unlike Strindberg's short piece, *The Stronger.* Each is a monologue in which the words of the one speaking actor skillfully suggest a complete drama that is over and done with. In the O'Neill play Mrs. Rowland lives with her husband Alfred in a dingy flat. She prepares breakfast, and talks to Alfred as he is making his toilet in the next room, complaining of her struggle to make ends meet, while he, "the millionaire Rowland's only son, the Harvard graduate, the poet, the catch of the town . . . ," goes off drinking and gallivanting. She taunts him for having married her and speaks in no uncertain terms of the girl he had really loved. Her wail swells to a climax, and subsides when she has no more to say. Silence. She waits for an answer—then the drip-drip of something in the bedroom. Alfred has cut his throat with a razor.

The Dreamy Kid, written at Provincetown in the summer of 1918, completes our record of O'Neill's one-act plays. This piece about Negroes is not one of his best: it is too obvious, too direct and melodramatic, to be very convincing. It tells of a murderer pursued by the police, who returns home to see his dying mother and gets caught.

As if to prove that he had not entirely lost interest in the one-act form, O'Neill allowed Frank Shay in 1924 to bring together four of his sea plays into a unified framework under the title S.S. *Glencairn.* These were *The Moon of the Caribbees, The Long Voyage Home, In the Zone,* and *Bound East for Cardiff.* The production, by Shay's Barnstormers of Provincetown, was so successful that it was taken over by the Jones-Macgowan-O'Neill combination at the Provincetown Playhouse in New York, where it ran for several weeks. The Provincetown Players revived the cycle early in 1929, using several of the actors who had played in the original productions.

In an interview (New York *Herald Tribune,* Nov. 16, 1924) O'Neill says of S.S. *Glencairn:*

". . . The individual plays·are complete in themselves, yet the identity of the crew goes through the series and welds the four one-acts into a long play. I do not claim any originality, though, for the idea, as Schnitzler has already done the same thing in *Anatol*. And doubtless others."

'Ile, The Moon, Bound East, and *The Long Voyage Home* were easily the most distinguished one-acters written up to that time by an American. During O'Neill's early years the short form sufficed for him: he had something to say, and he said it. When he was ready with a long play he was a full-fledged dramatist, not a writer of one-acters who expanded short pieces. *Beyond the Horizon* was full-grown; as a matter of fact, in its original form, it was over-grown.

BEYOND THE HORIZON

FIVE full-length plays preceded *Beyond the Horizon,* but not one of them has been preserved. Usually a sound and invariably an honest critic of his own work, O'Neill had made up his mind that he was going to keep nothing that did not represent the best that he had to give. The first I heard of *Beyond* was in a letter O'Neill wrote me in 1919:

"May I, when I retrieve a borrowed script, send you a copy of my long play, *Beyond the Horizon,* in the hope that you will give it a reading? This play is under contract for production by John D. Williams. It is a first serious attempt to do something bigger than my short plays express, and, because of my faith in its sincerity, I would like to submit it to you. I trust it would help to justify your kind encouragement of my work— an encouragement, I assure you, that means the devil of a lot to me."

The origin of the play, written at Provincetown in the winter of 1918, is explained in one of O'Neill's printed statements:

"I think," he writes, "the real life experience from which the idea of *Beyond the Horizon* sprang was this: On the British tramp steamer on which I made a voyage as ordinary seaman, Buenos Aires to New York, there was a Norwegian A.B., and we became quite good friends. The great sorrow and mistake of his life, he used to grumble, was that as a boy he had left the small paternal farm to run away to sea. He had been at sea twenty years, and had never gone home once in that time. . . . Yet he cursed the sea and the life it had led him—affectionately. He loved to hold forth on what a fool he had been to leave the farm. There was the life for you . . . at exactly the right moment . . . he turned up in my memory. I thought, 'What if he had stayed on the farm, with his instincts? What would have happened?' But I realized at once he never would have stayed. . . . It amused him to pretend he craved the farm. He was too harmonious a creature of the God of Things as They Are. . . . And from that point I started to think of a more intellectual, civilized type from the standpoint of the abovementioned God—a man who would have my Norwegian's inborn craving for the sea's unrest, only in him it would be conscious, too conscious, intellectually diluted into a vague, intangible wanderlust. His powers of resistance, both moral and physical, would also probably be correspondingly watered. He would throw away his instinctive dream and accept the thralldom of the farm for—why, for almost any nice little poetical craving—the romance of sex, say."

Robert Mayo is the victim of his dreams. As he is about to start on a long sea-voyage with his uncle, he believes he is desperately in love with the girl who is engaged to his brother Andrew; she impulsively throws Andrew over and accepts Robert, while Andrew sails in his place. Before long Ruth discovers that the marriage was a mistake and is sure that she is still in love with Andrew. Three years pass and Robert, ill and disillusioned, with only his child to comfort him, fails miserably in his efforts to make a go of the farm. Andrew comes back for a short time, only to bring unhappiness both to Ruth and to Robert: the woman realizes that he no longer loves her, and Robert, who had hoped to get from his brother at least a breath of the romance he himself had longed for, finds Andrew a commonplace and unimaginative materialist. From this point onward, Robert is the central figure. We are shown the mental and physical degeneration of a man who cannot live without illusions. Indeed, each character in the play is obsessed by his desire for what he can never have—for what lies beyond the horizon.

The play made something of an impression on the public. In spite of the uneven acting, the length of the manuscript—which was later cut—and of somewhat faulty direction, both critics and theater-goers were moved by the sincerity of the character-drawing in this grim tragedy of human futility. But there were few critics who gave O'Neill proper credit for his technical skill.

"You remember," he wrote me in March, 1920, "when you read *Beyond*, you remarked about its being an 'interesting technical experiment.' Why is it, I wonder, that not one other critic has given me credit for a deliberate departure in form in search of a greater flexibility? They have all accused me of bungling through ignorance—whereas, if I had wanted to, I could have laid the whole play in the farm interior, and made it tight as a drum a la Pinero. Then, too, I should imagine the symbolism I intended to convey by the alternating scenes would be apparent even from a glance at the program. It rather irks my professional pride, you see, to be accused of ignorance of conventional, everyday technique—I, a Baker 47 alumnus! Professor Baker himself, whose opinion in matters of technique I value as much as any man's . . . , has both read and seen *Beyond* and is delighted with and proud of it. He never mentioned my 'clumsiness.' Perhaps he saw it but appreciated the fact that it was intentional. Well, well, how I do go on! But I've been longing to protest about this to someone ever since I read the criticisms by really good critics who blamed my youthful inexperience—even for poor scenery and the interminable waits between the scenes!"

"I was forced," O'Neill said in 1927 when the play was revived, "to telescope the last scene of the final act into the first scene of the act," and though this was required because of scene-shifting difficulties back-stage, it was an improvement.

After all, there was nothing strikingly novel in the division of each act into two scenes, one indoors and one out-of-doors; it was a simple way of suggesting a tide-like rhythm in the lives of the characters.

Beyond the Horizon has, I think, been overpraised. For one thing, if produced exactly as it was written, it would require almost four hours to act. When O'Neill prepared it for republication some years after its first production, he reduced its bulk by at least one-fifth. Furthermore, it is too often unnecessarily violent and direct in action and speech; the hand of the dramatist is too much in evidence: he pauses too often to direct our attention to what he is doing, and what his people are thinking, a fault that in some of his later plays he sometimes carries to extremes. He had not quite the courage or the skill to let his characters develop themselves.

A few months after this play appeared O'Neill received the Pulitzer Prize. "When my wife wired me the news," he told me, "I thought it meant maybe some wooden medal or other, until a friend told me it was a thousand dollars. Then I came to, and paid off some of my worst debts!"

CHRIS CHRISTOPHERSON

ONLY a few weeks after I had heard of *Beyond* I learned that O'Neill was busy with his next script. In June he wrote that his agent, Richard J. Madden, had sold the "latest play, *Chris Christopherson*, which I completed this spring. . . . I would like very much to have you read *Chris*. It is a sea play—a character study of an old Swede. May I send you a copy when I get one? At present the agent and Tyler have all the scripts."

This earlier version of the play that was later to become *Anna Christie* I have never seen, but shortly after the production O'Neill wrote me:

> "My other play, *Chris*, which opened in Atlantic City two weeks ago, is not faring very well financially and I doubt if it will come to New York under its present management. I am just as well pleased. They cut it unmercifully in my enforced absence—on the strength of an adverse decision by an Atlantic City audience, at that!—and little play is left, I guess. It is in six scenes—another experiment—and the curtain rings down before 10:30—after the cutting. You can imagine the movie effect. I'm too disgusted to witness a performance, but my agent and friends in Philly have reported to me. The play is also miserably cast. As it is a character sketch built up bit by bit you can understand what the rough methods they used accomplished. I hope you'll be able to read this play some day soon. I know it has its faults, but I still think it doesn't deserve its present fate, and, if treated sympathetically, would find its public as *Beyond* has."

Chris was never published. After the tryout in Atlantic City and Philadelphia it closed, to appear later, after a great deal of revision and rewriting, as *Anna Christie*.

THE STRAW

The Straw comes next in order of composition. It was written at Provincetown in 1918 and 1919. This is a love story about an Irish girl who meets a young newspaperman at a tuberculosis sanatorium. After a few months Stephen leaves, completely cured, ready to make his way as a writer, while Eileen, whose well-being depends wholly upon Stephen, remains. She has only him to live for, and when he returns to see her later on—no longer in love—she loses courage. In his masculine way Stephen makes a brave pretense, trying to give Eileen a "straw" of hope. It is not stated in so many words whether

Eileen believes him or not; that is not necessary. It is only a matter of time before she will learn the truth.

Once again, as in *Beyond the Horizon*, the playwright presents a set of characters who base their lives on illusions. Sometimes this takes the form of a dream of beauty, sometimes it is love, sometimes physical passion. In the later plays we find Ponce de Leon in quest of the illusion of love and fame, Marco Polo after the illusion of power, Lazarus after a solution of the problem of life everlasting, and Reuben Light in *Dynamo* after a religion that he can believe in; but always it is the quest that counts—the pursuit that never ends, the search for happiness, the hope for an ultimate meaning.

In *The Straw* there is little of the kind of exposition that sometimes interferes with the satisfactory development of O'Neill's themes, although toward the end is a passage, brief in itself but giving point to the play without throwing it out of key. Stephen asks the superintendent why they have been given a "hopeless hope," and Miss Gilpin tells him: "Isn't everything we know—just that—when you think of it? (*Her face lighting up with a consoling revelation.*) But there must be something back of it—some promise of fulfillment— somehow—somewhere—in the spirit of hope itself."

In this play the dramatist has thrown together two young people face to face with the realities of love and passion and death. Love is a hopeless hope and so is life, yet there must be a reason. "Come, now," says Stephen, "confess, damn it! There's always hope, isn't there? What do you know? Can you say you know anything?"

The Straw is filled with a questioning perplexity, a youthful exasperation in the presence of suffering and death. There seems no reason for it all, yet there is the no less perplexing fact of hope, the presence of which seems to proclaim some pattern or intention in the scheme of the universe. Later, in *Desire Under the Elms*, *The Fountain*, and *The Iceman Cometh*, O'Neill was again to envisage the tragedy of futility, the heartbreaking failure of man under the pressure of inexplicable forces, yet triumphing not in spite of but because of the obstacles that seem to be, but are not really, tragic in a conventional and material sense. It is for this reason that I have always considered O'Neill at bottom an optimist, a yea-sayer. He never leaves us feeling that life is not worth living. If he were as pessimistic as he is often said to be, in the first place he would not have gone to the trouble of trying to prove the futility of existence. Consider the endings of his plays; are they not usually pointed with the expression of hope, even a "hopeless hope"? As a matter of fact, a fairly good case might be made out against O'Neill for reading the riddles of life a little too easily.

The Straw was not successful in the theater. I think it was too painful to please the average playgoer, and possibly too much a love story to please those who don't like to be called "average." Also, in laying the scene in a sanatorium for tuber-cular patients the playwright risked losing the normal point of view. His use of disease as an element of plot, unless it can be shown as a necessary thing (as in *Ghosts*), is a little unfair.

THE EMPEROR JONES

THE production of *The Emperor Jones* in 1920 established O'Neill as a "regular" dramatist. It was written the same year at Provincetown. This play, effectively mounted, well directed, and imaginatively acted by the colored actor Charles Gilpin, was a popular success, and has been often revived both with Paul Robeson and again with Gilpin.

As pure "theater" *The Emperor Jones* is one of the best of all the O'Neill plays, though most of it is only a dramatic monologue. It is a kind of unfolding, in reverse order, of the tragical epic of the American Negro.

O'Neill has told the story of the play's origin in an inter-view printed in the New York *World* of Nov. 9, 1924:

"The idea of *The Emperor Jones* came from an old circus man I knew. This man told me a story current in Hayti concerning the late President Sam. This was to the effect that Sam had said they'd never get him with a lead bullet; that he would get himself first with a silver one. . . . This notion about the silver bullet struck me, and I made a note of the story. About six months later I got the idea of the woods, but I couldn't see how it could be done on the stage, and I passed it up again. A year elapsed. One day I was reading of the religious feasts in the Congo and the uses to which the drum is put there: how it starts at a normal pulse and is slowly intensified until the heartbeat of everyone present corresponds to the frenzied beat of the drum. There was an idea and an experiment. How would this sort of thing work on an audience in a theater? The effect of the tropical forest on the human imagination was honestly come by. It was the result of my own experience while prospecting for gold in Spanish Honduras."

The play is composed of a very few simple elements—a hunted man, a series of sharply defined pictures, and a monotonous rhythmical drumbeat (a device used by Austin Strong in his melodrama *The Drums of Oude* in 1906). *The Emperor Jones* is a magnificent presentment of panic fear in the breast of a half-civilized Negro.

In stating my belief that it is not so fine a play as *Desire Under the Elms* or *Mourning Becomes Electra*, I am not belittling the virtues of *The Emperor Jones*. It is beautifully and completely what O'Neill intended it to be; if it is not in all ways comparable to the best of the later plays it is because in the last analysis it deals with obvious forces in an obvious way. It is not built upon harmonies but on a single theme, directly stated and reiterated a trifle monotonously. The play reveals itself at once, not indirectly, insinuatingly, suggestively, progressively.

Am I captious in asking that *The Emperor Jones* should suggest more than the dramatist aimed at? I hardly think so. O'Neill is not merely a dramatist; if he were, this book would never have been written: he is at his best an artist who uses the theater as a medium for the expression of his attitude toward life in terms of human character. I grant that *The Emperor Jones* is a fine achievement, but it does not belong in the highest rank of the writer's works.

THE FAILURE OF *GOLD*

Gold, written at Provincetown in 1920, does not "come off," but what a magnificent idea there is in it! Because of the limitations of the dramatic form O'Neill could not, at least he did not, create a background on the huge scale of his conception: he was compelled to people his stage with characters most of whom are conventional and commonplace. Captain Bartlett, cast ashore on a desert island with some of his crew, is a party to the murder of two of his men. He had discovered what he believes to be treasure, and crazed by thirst and a prey to suspicion, he allows the crime to be committed. But already corrupted by his lust for gold, he tries to evade his moral responsibilities. The Captain and his companions are rescued, and the next act finds them, six months later, at his home on the California coast. Bartlett has fitted out another ship and is about to sail off once more in quest of the treasure. His wife Sarah, ill and fearing that all is not well, opposes the venture. His son Nat, who has gradually learned the facts, is seized with the madness that is consuming his father. He wants to sail with the Captain. As if to strengthen his own faith in his quest, the Captain forces Sarah, ill as she is, to christen the ship. The next day his two companions conspire to sail without him and make off with the gold themselves. But they need a captain. Young Drew, engaged to Bartlett's daughter Sue, is persuaded to go with them in Bartlett's interest, and when the Captain is at home they sail off, while the old man stands on the hill cursing them.

The last act takes place a year later. It is a rewritten version of the one-acter *Where the Cross Is Made.* In fact, O'Neill

calls the entire work "an elaboration of an early one-act play."
The schooner has been lost at sea, and the Captain, now
wholly in the grip of hallucinations, is only the shadow of his
old self. He is pursued by the fantoms of his victims and the
ineradicable belief that his schooner is on the point of returning, laden with gold. His passion for the treasure has meantime killed his wife and driven Nat mad. At the very end he
produces a sample of the "gold" he has kept by him in secret,
but Nat in a lucid interval realizes that it is only junk. The
Captain tears up the map showing where the treasure is
buried, and dies.

Here is a particularly interesting idea, a broad canvas, a
plot with infinite possibilities, and characters susceptible of
treatment in the grand manner. But *Gold* is not much more
than a courageous attempt. Captain Bartlett is no mean snivel-
ing coward: he is potentially a Balzacian giant, a Grandet, a
Gobseck. Up to the end of the play he is treated from a rigidly
realistic standpoint. His venture is in its way heroic; his crimes
should be treated heroically, because his quest was a splendid
dream. His remorse should be commensurate with his moral
stature.

Now if I am wrong, and O'Neill aimed at portraying no
more than a petty adventurer, then the whole idea of *Gold* is
hardly worth treating. But I am sure he was aiming at something bigger than that, and I suspect that he was simply not
equal to his theme. The play, as written, seems to be the dramatization of an idea, not a living organism. Instead of allowing the characters to go their way and create their own situations, O'Neill guided and directed them, and in default of
that white heat which welds together such elements as O'Neill
has imagined, he resorts to the feeble expedient of explanation. Time and again his characters stop to tell us what they
are doing and why, instead of going ahead and doing it. In no
other early play are his basic shortcomings as a playmaker
more strikingly evident.

AN AUSTRIAN POET ON O'NEILL

HUGO VON HOFMANNSTHAL, in one of the most acute criticisms of O'Neill yet written, takes the American to task for this very fault. "It is," he writes in *The Freeman* of March 21, 1923, "a little disappointing to a European with his complex background to see the arrow strike the target toward which he has watched it speeding all the while." Elsewhere in the same article he adds: "The reason for this general weakness is, I think, that the dramatist, unable to make his dialogue a complete expression of human motives, is forced at the end simply to squeeze it out like a wet sponge."

ANNA CHRISTIE

I HAVE said before that *Anna Christie* (final version written at Provincetown in the summer of 1920) was the outgrowth of an earlier play, *Chris*, or *Chris Christopherson*. It was also at one time called *De Old Davil*. This most widely popular of all his early plays seems to have given the dramatist a good deal of trouble. Just how to end it was one of his biggest problems, as we shall see.

In its final version *Anna Christie* is a play about a woman. It was in the beginning a play about the woman's father.

I have already told about Jimmy the Priest's where O'Neill lived for a while in New York. It was there that he met the man who became Chris Christopherson. In fact, the two were room-mates. I quote again from the New York *Times* article of Dec. 21, 1924:

> "He had sailed the sea until he was sick of the mention of it. But it was the only work he knew. At the time he was my room-mate he was out of work, wouldn't go to sea and spent the time guzzling whiskey and razzing the sea. In time he got a coal barge to captain. One Christmas Eve he got terribly

drunk and tottered away about 2 o'clock in the morning for his barge. The next morning he was found frozen on a cake of ice between the piles and the dock. In trying to board the barge he stumbled on the plank and fell over."

The story tells of the regeneration of Anna under the influence of the sea and the love of a man. It is not until long after her arrival at Jimmy the Priest's that her father learns she has been living for a time as a prostitute. But it is made clear—it is at least asserted and reiterated—that she has preserved a virginal soul, and when she confesses to Burke that she never really loved any man before she met him, we are willing to believe her—at the time. Living happily on her father's barge, she is ready for a "pure" love when her hero emerges out of the blackness of the fog. Their passion develops rapidly up to the point where Anna confesses; then the man reacts, instinctively rebelling against the idea of marrying the kind of woman he had been used to hiring on occasion. But after getting drunk he returns to her, and the two are united.

Now for O'Neill's problem. Here are a few sentences from a letter written to George Jean Nathan in 1921, and first published in Isaac Goldberg's *Theatre of George Jean Nathan* (New York, 1926):

"Your criticism certainly probes the vital spot. The devil of it is, I don't see my way out. From the middle of the third act I feel the play ought to be dominated by the woman's psychology, and I have a conviction that dumb people of her sort, unable to voice strong, strange feelings, the emotions can find outlet only through the language and gestures of the heroics in the novels and movies they are familiar with—that is, that in moments of great stress life copies melodrama. Anna forced herself on me, middle of third act, at her most theatric. In real life I felt she would unconsciously be compelled, through sheer inarticulateness, to the usual 'big scene' and wait hopefully for her happy ending. And as she is the only one of the three who knows exactly what she wants, she would get it. And the sea outside—life—waits. The happy ending is merely the comma at the end of a gaudy introductory clause, with the body of the sentence still unwritten. (In fact, I once thought of calling the play *Comma*.) Of course, this sincerity of life pent up in the trappings of theater is impossible to project clearly, I guess. The two things cancel and negate each other, resulting, as you have said, in a seeming H. A. Jones compromise. Yet it is queerly fascinating to me because I believe it's a new, true, angle."

O'Neill clearly saw his difficulty. The projection of "sincerity of life" was his problem in *Anna Christie*, but when he was writing the play he discovered that plot—"trappings of theater"—unless determined and shaped by character, may become the arch-enemy of character. His plot was to some extent predetermined, but when he got deeper into the heart and mind of Anna he found that he must falsify either one thing or the other; character, or the plot as he had outlined it. But the trouble lay still deeper: from the very beginning he had made the mistake of not deciding exactly whose play it was to be, Anna's or Chris's. Out of this confusion came the rebelliousness of his plot before he finished with it. He found his flesh-and-blood people chafing under the restraint of "theater," which means that his knowledge of people was at that moment clearer than his knowledge of play-construction. The diverse elements are not completely fused, and while the result is momentarily and superficially effective, it is not wholly convincing as an interpretation of character. The play won popular success because of its intrinsic effectiveness in separate scenes, and as a whole because of its somewhat threadbare but always "safe" philosophy.

In the letter to Nathan, O'Neill admits he is afraid he hasn't made his "comma" clear:

"My ending seems to have a false definiteness about it that is misleading—a happy-ever-after which I did not intend. I relied on the father's last speech of superstitious uncertainty to let my theme flow through and on. It does not do this rightly. I now have the stoker not entirely convinced by the oath of a non-Catholic, although he is forced by his great want to accept her in spite of this. In short, that all of them at the end have a vague foreboding that, although they have had their moment, the decision still rests with the sea which has achieved the conquest of Anna."

What O'Neill may not have seen was that the union of two lovers *is* a happy ending, no matter what is hinted at regarding their future.[1] This is not only a convention of the theater, it is a psychological fact, because for the time being a man and a woman in love are usually—or presumably—happy at the prospect of marriage. *They* don't know what's coming, and the audience don't care, so what difference if the kill-joy author shouts aloud that all is not well? He no doubt felt that in life Anna and Burke would, under the circumstances, marry, and he was quite right in closing his play with that situation. But at the same time he didn't want to write the usual play about a prostitute "purified" by love; that seemed too conventional, so he took a woman who was really not a prostitute at all, but a normal healthy girl who drifted almost by accident into a profession that was distasteful to her. She is capable of love, and we are sure there is nothing vicious in her at all.

But is not this a fatal weakness in the play? For purposes of dramatic effect she is at first shown to be a vulgar, cynical street-walker; at the proper moment she breaks down and confesses to her lover, and after it has been asserted that she is really "pure" in soul she is ready to marry the "hero." In this way the playwright tried to do more than he legitimately could do: shock us by the spectacle of conventional "sin," and then turn round and ask us to forget it. No, Anna is by no means consistent. Human nature and dramatic technique are not quite reconciled.

[1] In his long letter to the *Times* (Dec. 16, 1921), O'Neill argues the point in detail. He says . . . "Meaning that I wish it understood as unhappy? Meaning nothing of the kind. Meaning what I have said before, that the play has no ending. . . . The curtain falls. Behind it their lives go on."

Fundamentally, the point of the play is obscured. If Anna were really affected by her new life it is necessary that she should undergo some radical conversion beyond that brought about by her passion for Burke; but since she never was a real daughter of joy her only problem is the minor one of readjustment to a life in circumstances different from what she had been used to. Supposing, however, that she had been really vicious, that—though she had never loved any man she met in the way of business—she had had to fight the allurements of the flesh, would not this have been the basis for a more sincere and effective drama? As it is, the issue is only too clear and the struggle not particularly worth showing. In fact, there is scarcely any struggle at all.

Anna Christie was not conceived in its entirety, or rather it was conceived as at least two separate plays. The first act, for instance, is exceptionally good, though not the height of perfection that many critics declare it to be; the characterization of Chris—except for over-insistence on the "ole davil sea" motif—is admirable; the dialogue on the whole is better than anything, except in *The Moon of the Caribbees* and *'Ile*, the playwright had written up to that time. But in spite of some of the most skillful play-writing that we have seen on our stage, *Anna Christie* is basically not right.

DIFF'RENT

THE somber two-act play, *Diff'rent*, written at Provincetown in 1920, was never a great success in the theater, even with the help of the censor who tried to stop it in New York, and there are few, even among O'Neill's admirers, who care much for it. It was not received very favorably, and shortly after the opening O'Neill wrote to Nathan about the poor "press."

He said: "Well, this is rather reassuring. I had begun to think I was too popular to be honest."

In this play O'Neill shows a firm grasp on his situation; he knew his characters and was able to make them speak and act, not according to a scenario, but as they would act in life.

Emma Crosby learns that Caleb Williams, a sea captain to whom she is engaged, has had an affair with a native woman in the South Sea Islands. She has always believed him sexually pure, "diff'rent" from other men, and the shock of the discovery causes her to break off the engagement. The second act is in Emma's home thirty years later. Emma is an embittered victim of sex-suppression. Caleb's nephew, Benny, an American doughboy who fought in World War I, recently returned from France, is deliberately "stringing" the old maid in order to get money out of her.

The pitiful Emma is gradually drawn into the snare set by the heartless doughboy, and deceived into believing that the youth is going to marry her. The steps by which Emma approaches the sweet discussion of sex are shown with such skill that the ridiculous old woman becomes an almost tragic figure. The repressions of a lifetime are in one brief moment brought to the surface.

Emma's disillusion is swift and cruel. In spite of what Caleb and her relatives have told her, she clings to her absurd illusion. "Just because I'm a mite older'n him," she tells Caleb, "can't them things happen jist as well as any other—what d'you suppose—can't I care for him same as any woman cares for a man? But I do! I care more'n I ever did for you!" It is Benny who deals the final blow: if his uncle buys him off, he will promise not to carry out his threat of marrying. "Say, honest, Aunt Emmer, you didn't believe—you didn't think I was really stuck on you, did you? Aw, say, how could I? Have a heart! Why, you're as old as ma is. Ain't you, Aunt Emmer? (*He adds ruthlessly.*) And I'll say you look it, too!"

The end of the play is needlessly violent. Caleb hangs himself, and the moment Emma learns of it she "moves like a sleepwalker toward the door," murmuring, "Wait, Caleb, I'm going down to the barn"—to put an end to herself.

MURDER AND SUICIDE

MURDER and suicide, which are easy devices in the hands of a capable dramatist, should be sparingly used in the theater. Physical violence loses much of its tragic impact unless it is shown to be inescapable. It is a quick way out for the playwright who doesn't know what else to do or, with a more conscientious artist, an equally easy way of bringing his plot to a full stop.

In *Diff'rent*, though O'Neill shows both Caleb and Emma driven to extremes, I am not convinced that they would commit suicide. There are many people who either dare not, or perhaps don't want to, kill themselves—even though they believe they have nothing more to live for—people who go on living in quiet desperation. Caleb and Emma are like that. To kill them off at the end is an act of mercy, and O'Neill's mood here was anything but merciful: he is after the truth. It will be noticed that in *Desire Under the Elms*, where the tragedy is more bitter and the passion deeper, there is no suicide, though all three of the principal characters are even more clearly justified in killing themselves than Caleb and Emma are. They go on living. "Life doesn't end," says O'Neill. "One experience is but the birth of another." Violent death is seldom the solution of anything, in life or in fiction. It is too often a makeshift device. Do you remember Lessing's anecdote? A spectator at a play asked his neighbor what a certain character died of. "Of the fifth act," was the reply, and Lessing adds that in "very truth the fifth act is an ugly disease that carries off many a one to whom the first four acts promised a longer life."

THE QUEST FOR NEW FORMS

IT IS not strange that a young and ambitious playwright, especially if he is interested in saying something about life, should concern himself with problems of technique. But many skilled playwrights, having learned to handle the tools of their trade, are content to use them over and over again. O'Neill seems, however, to have been driven by some inner necessity to devise a whole new set of tools every time he planned a new work, as though its implications and its physical shape could not be fitted into any mould he had already used.

Being in no sense a purveyor of theatrical commodities, he takes an artist's delight in facing new difficulties. An obstacle easily overcome is an obstacle scarcely worth attacking. But there is more to this than the joy of the craftsman. O'Neill is always striving to show his characters and develop his situations in the most emphatic manner possible, to dig down as deep into their souls as he can, and to exhibit only what he considers really important. There is no one way of doing this: "technique" for such a man is a barren and meaningless bit of jargon. "If I thought there was only one way," he said some years ago, "I should be following the mechanistic creed —which is the very thing I condemn." Each new play demands its own specially articulated structure. Surface realism suffices for one set of characters, old-fashioned romance for another, and so on.

Some years ago several young Germans popularized a mechanical sort of technique known as "Expressionism." The term was applied both to the plays and to the physical means used in mounting them. It is an outgrowth of certain devices used by Strindberg and Wedekind. "Expressionism" in drama is a misleading term. It is not radically different from what most artists have used in one way or another from the earliest times.

THE HAIRY APE

SOME critics have called O'Neill an Expressionist, because *The Hairy Ape* and, in another way, *The Emperor Jones*, resemble certain plays of Toller, Hasenclever, Kaiser and other so-called

Expressionists. It is also asserted that he has been considerably influenced by the young Germans. I asked him once what he knew about the recent dramatic developments in Middle Europe, and whether he had consciously made use of the methods of Kaiser and the rest.

FOREIGN INFLUENCES

"THE first Expressionistic play that I ever saw," he answered, "was Kaiser's *From Morn to Midnight*, produced in New York in 1922, after I'd written both *The Emperor Jones* and *The Hairy Ape*. I had read *From Morn to Midnight* before *The Hairy Ape* was written, but not before the idea for it was planned. The point is that *The Hairy Ape* is a direct descendant of *Jones*, written long before I had ever heard of Expressionism, and its form needs no explanation but this. As a matter of fact, I did not think much of *Morn to Midnight*, and still don't. It is too easy. It would not have influenced me." Whether he had read or heard about Kaiser's *Gas* trilogy I can't say, but *Dynamo* offers certain parallels to that remarkable work.

Writing about *The Hairy Ape* fifteen years after it was produced he said that "its manner is inseparable from its matter, and it found its form as a direct descendant from *The Emperor Jones*."

In a letter to Charles O'Brien Kennedy, who directed the revival of *The Moon of the Caribbees* at the Provincetown Playhouse, O'Neill wrote in 1921: "Well, I'm hard at work at *The Hairy Ape*, and it is coming along in great shape. I've got the swing of it now, I think. Believe me, it's going to be strong stuff with a kick in each mit—and stuff done in a new way, along the lines of *Emperor Jones* in construction but even more so. You can tell Wolheim for me that the lead will be a bigger part than Brutus Jones. If I could go ahead without interruption, I think I'd have the whole thing completed

—in long hand—by the first of the year. [It was, as a matter of record, completed in December of 1921.] But, darn it, the chances are I'll have to go down to New York for a few days to see my mother and Jim. . . . But, whatever interrupts, I've got my strangle hold on the play now and the rest is only a a question of how soon.''

In order to satisfy myself that I was not inventing evidence after the fact, I remembered having written in 1922 that the three writers who most directly affected the dramatists of Young Germany were Nietzsche, Strindberg and Wedekind. To anyone who has read this far it will be clear that Nietzsche, Strindberg and Wedekind—particularly the first two—were among the most powerful influences on the youthful Eugene O'Neill. Like Hasenclever and the others, he too had felt the futility of trying to express in the old forms the multifariousness of modern life, but, unlike them, he based his work to a great extent on human character—not the type or the abstraction. Yet *The Hairy Ape* is something of an exception. Instead of intensifying a particular man, he has symbolized him in the person of Yank.

"*The Hairy Ape,*" he said in the New York *Herald Tribune* (Nov. 16, 1924), "was propaganda in the sense that it was a symbol of man, who has lost his old harmony with nature, the harmony which he used to have as an animal and has not yet acquired in a spiritual way. Thus, not being able to find it on earth nor in heaven, he's in the middle, trying to make peace, taking the 'woist punches from bot' of 'em.' This idea was expressed in Yank's speech. The public saw just the stoker, not the symbol, and the symbol makes the play either important or just another play. Yank can't go forward, and so he tries to go back. This is what his shaking hands with the gorilla meant. But he can't go back to 'belonging' either. The gorilla kills him. The subject here is the same ancient one that always was and always will be the one subject for drama, and that is man and his struggle with his own fate. The struggle used to be with the gods, but is now with himself, his own past, his attempt 'to belong.' "

An intellectual concept, you see, underlies *The Hairy Ape,* a philosophy growing not out of a single human situation but from certain deductions made by the dramatist about life and society. The idea sprang, however, from a decidedly human situation:

> "I shouldn't have known the stokers if I hadn't happened to scrape an acquaintance with one of our own furnace room gang at Jimmy the Priest's. His name was Driscoll, and he was a Liverpool Irishman . . . the synonym for a tough customer . . . Driscoll . . . came to a strange end. He committed suicide by jumping overboard in mid-ocean. . . . Why? It was the why of Driscoll's suicide that gave me the germ of the idea. . . ."
> (From *The American Magazine,* Nov., 1922.)

The idea was good, and the play is one of the most interesting of all O'Neill's works. It is a series of short scenes, beginning in the hold of the steamer where Yank then "belongs," and ending in the Zoo, where he is killed, and "at last belongs" —"perhaps."

The play holds you by its tragic irony, its novelty, its underlying idea, its strange settings; your curiosity is aroused at the beginning, and not fully satisfied even at the end. But in the last analysis it remains largely a philosophical and therefore an impersonal work. O'Neill at one time clearly realized that a play lives by reason of its human appeal. In the article quoted on page 84 he says: "I personally do not believe that an idea can be readily put over to an audience except through characters. When it sees 'A Man' and 'A Woman'—just abstractions, it loses the human contact by which it identifies itself with the protagonist of the play . . . the character of Yank remains a man and everyone recognizes him as such." He sees that there is no such thing as an abstract plot in life, and that only human beings, artfully manipulated by a craftsman, can make one.

Yet I think O'Neill is mistaken in believing that Yank "remains a man." He has human attributes, it is true, but "he is a symbol." Is it possible to make a man and a symbol at the same time? A human being, like Hamlet, may "symbolize" certain qualities or characteristics or even sum up a whole philosophy, but when the dramatist deliberately uses a figure in order to make him typify man, or humanity, he necessarily minimizes the human elements in his story. At least I feel this is true in the case of Yank. He is supernatural, more or less an abstraction, an idea. Could it be otherwise, granted the dramatist's aim?

Still, O'Neill could hardly have used the same direct and realistic methods that served him in *Diff'rent*. I believe he might have made his points just as well by keeping the whole play out of the realm of the supernatural. I have used the term supernaturalism, and in turning to O'Neill's note on Strindberg in a program of the Provincetown Playhouse, I find him speaking of it in a passage that explains his viewpoint in writing *The Hairy Ape*.

SUPERNATURALISM

"Yet it is only by means of some form of 'supernaturalism' that we may express in the theater what we comprehend intuitively of that self-obsession which is the particular discount we moderns have to pay for the loan of life. The old 'naturalism'—or 'realism,' if you prefer (I would to God some genius were gigantic enough to define clearly the separateness of these terms once and for all!)—no longer applies. It represents our fathers' daring aspirations toward self-recognition by holding the family kodak up to ill-nature. But to us their old audacity is *blague*, we have taken too many snapshots of each other in every graceless position. We have endured too much from the banality of surfaces."

It is surely possible to write a play—even a supernatural play—about recognizably human beings and dispense entirely with the banality of surfaces, but you cannot very well have

your human beings serve these two purposes at the same time.
Yank cannot symbolize man and his efforts to "belong," and
remain a single individual. He might have been a man and
still have embodied the dramatist's ideas; he might have been
treated, like Ephraim in *Desire Under the Elms*, as a man
from whose character we are allowed to make deductions and
generalizations, but he is not so treated. It is for this reason
that *The Hairy Ape*, for all its appeal, remains a rather cold
bit of dramatized philosophy.

The Hairy Ape, *The First Man* and *The Fountain* were all
written in 1921. A symbolic fantasy, half realistic and half
grotesque, a realistic middle-class satire, and a romantic play
—all from the pen of the "morbid" O'Neill, and in the same
year!

THE FIRST MAN

The First Man was not a success on the stage, and it is usually
regarded as one of O'Neill's least happy efforts. It is a most
ambitious failure. The play presents the struggle of a high-
minded scientist to live up to his ideals. He is about to set
forth on an expedition in search of the earliest traces of man,
and he has with the utmost difficulty arranged to have his
wife accompany him on his five years' quest. Two years before
they had lost their children under tragic circumstances and
made up their minds not to have any more. Their lives will be
wholly devoted to Curtis Jayson's work.

As the play opens the Jaysons are faced with a problem that
is to end in tragedy: Martha is going to have a baby. Curt is
thunderstruck; his career and life-work are threatened, and
the worst of it is that Martha seems happy. "Oh, Curt," she
says, "I wish I could tell you what I feel, make you feel with
me the longing for a child. If you had just the tiniest bit of
feminine in you—! . . . But you're so utterly masculine, dear!
That's what has made me love you, I suppose—so I've no

right to complain of it . . . I don't. I wouldn't have you changed one bit! I love you. And I love the things you love—your work—because it's a part of you. And that's what I want you to do—to reciprocate—to love the creator in me—to desire that I, too, should complete myself with the thing nearest my heart!"

The dilemma is perhaps even too clearly stated in this speech. Both Curt and Martha are intelligent; they understand each other and, except in this one case, each sympathizes with the other's point of view. Then comes the explanation:

"It's all my fault," says Martha, "I've spoiled you by giving up my life so completely to yours. You've forgotten I've one. Oh, I don't mean that I was a martyr. I know that in you alone lay my happiness in these years—after the children died. But we are no longer what we were then. We must, both of us, relearn to love and respect—what we have become."

He will not yet face the issue squarely; but he does love her:

> MARTHA—(*In a whisper*). Yes, you love me. But who am I? You don't know.
> CURT—(*Frightfully*). Martha! Stop! This is terrible. (*They continue to be held by each other's fearfully questioning eyes.*)

And the curtain falls on the second act. The third is concerned with the birth of Martha's child. Curt's attitude has not changed: he hates the child that has ruined his work, and Martha has read that hatred in his eyes. That is why Martha is suffering so long and so cruelly. "I was holding her hands," says Curt, "and her eyes searched mine with such a longing question in them—and she read only my hatred there, not my love for her." Then Martha dies, after giving birth to a boy. This scene is played to the accompaniment of the bickerings of hypocritical relatives, and the sympathetic Richard Bigelow, friend and confidant of Curt and his wife. Curt's brothers, sisters, in-laws, and the rest—products of middle-class morality—furnish a complex basis for the main theme in their attempts to make a scandal by fixing the paternity of the child upon Bigelow. The suspicions of these people are so fantastic that Curt has no notion of their tenor until the play has almost ended. Up to the moment when the truth dawns on him, his relatives are only more or less disagreeable irritants. To make matters worse, Curt is so "hardened" in their eyes that he refuses to see the baby; a final "proof" that the child is not his. He then announces his intention of going away, but this evidence of his callousness is just too much for the family to take:

> ESTHER—Yes, you really must think of us, Curt.
> CURT—But—I—you—how are you concerned? Pretense? You mean you want me to stay and pretend—in order that you won't be disturbed by any silly tales they tell about me? (*With a wild laugh.*) Good God, this is too much! Why does a man have to be maddened by fools at such a time! (*Raging.*) Leave me alone! You're like a swarm of poisonous flies.

When at last he understands what they are driving at, he dashes up, sees the baby and returns to address the assembled family: ". . . I'll come back (*the light of an ideal beginning to shine in his eyes*). When he's old enough, I'll teach him to know and love a big, free life. Martha used to say that he would take her place in time. Martha shall live again for me and him."

The idea of the play is formulaic: a man whose dreams are ruined—or so he believes—pulled back to earth by the demands of life; and at last given a new impetus. The never-ending aspirations of man. The undying hope of the individual and his ultimate identification with life through something larger than himself. It is the same in *Desire Under the Elms, The Fountain,* and *The Great God Brown.* But the method used here in different. There is far too much discussion of abstract ideas: O'Neill seems unable to allow his people to be themselves; they must constantly talk over the why and the wherefore.

WELDED AND THE PROBLEM OF MARRIAGE

Welded was written at Ridgefield in 1923. This is the most compact, the most deliberately and exclusively intellectual of all the O'Neill plays. It is a work of hard surfaces; the study of a man and woman hopelessly linked together by bonds of passion.

A sensitive man and his equally sensitive wife are tortured on the one hand by their love for each other, and on the other by an almost psychopathic passion for self-torture. Michael Cape has the "forehead of a thinker, the eyes of a dreamer, the nose and mouth of a sensualist." Eleanor's face is "dominated by passionate, blue-gray eyes. . . . The first impression of her whole personality is one of charm partly innate, partly imposed by years of self-discipline."

Says the woman: "Our ideal was difficult. (*Sadly.*) Sometimes I think we've demanded too much. Now there's nothing left but that something which can't give itself. And I blame you for this—because I can neither take more nor give more —and you blame me (*She smiles tenderly.*) and then we fight!"

Their life together is a rhythmical ebb and flow of love and strife. The play begins to move on the eve of a crisis. The excuse—for something must start the trouble—is jealousy: Michael is jealous of Eleanor's supposed affection for John, a situation which began years before their marriage. He cannot remain satisfied with things as they are: he is a sensitive and introspective artist, given to analyzing himself and his relations with his wife, while she is jealous of his work.

The situation tightens as each seems determined to kill his love for the other. Michael goes out, and Eleanor cries after him: "Go! Go! I'm glad! I hate you. I'll go too! I'm free! I'll go—!"

The second act is in two scenes, the first of which is in John's house. Eleanor arrives, and throws herself into her friend's arms, but she is unable to carry out her intentions. There is something in her heart that cannot be killed. "My love for him is my own, not his! That he can never possess!" And she returns home.

The second scene is the shabby bedroom of a prostitute. Michael has gone there with the first woman he has picked up, but he is no better able to carry out his intention than Eleanor was. "I can't!" he tells the woman. "I can't. I'm the weaker. Our love must live on in me. There's no death for it. There's no freedom—while I live."

The last act is in the Capes' home again. Eleanor and Michael "smile with a queer understanding. They act for the moment like two persons of different races, deeply in love but separated by a barrier of language." They realize that they are "welded," indissolubly linked together. It's a fact they both face, and in facing it frankly and understandingly they are given a glimmer of hope. "They stare into each other's eyes. It is as if now by a sudden flash from within they recognized themselves, shorn of all the ideas, attitudes, cheating gestures which constitute the vanity of personality. Everything, for this second, becomes simple for them—serenely unquestionable. It becomes impossible that they should ever deny life, through each other, again."

They are strong, and they can live again. "But we'll hate," says Michael, while Eleanor echoes, "Yes!"

> CAPE—And we'll torture and tear, and clutch for each other's souls,—fight—fail and hate again—(*He raises his voice in aggressive triumph.*)—but—fail with pride—with joy!"

Shortly after the play closed I asked O'Neill what the trouble was. "The actors," he answered, "did about as well as they could, but the whole point of the play was lost in the production. The most significant thing in the last act was the silences between the speeches. What was actually spoken should have served to a great extent just to punctuate the meaningful pauses. The actors didn't get that."

The stage-directions show what the dramatist is driving at, but no dramatist can afford to leave too much to any actor: the actor is—he must be—the more or less inspired servant and mouthpiece of the author, and it is the author's business to give him the necessary lines to speak and business to act out. Michael tells Eleanor that he has tried hard to express to her all that he feels, but in the end he can "only stutter like an idiot!" It was O'Neill's problem to make the idiotic stutterings of his character express something that mattered and give some relevancy to the human problem he tried to dramatize. That is the function of dialogue. This last act is too meager: too much is suggested in the directions, which are a commentary rather than a guide, and too little in the dialogue. It is rather a large order to ask any actor and actress to reveal, without words, the fact for instance that it "becomes impossible that they should ever deny life, through each other, again."

What is true of the last act applies with almost equal force to the others. The play is not intended as surface realism: it is an attempt to strip away all the non-essentials, to reveal directly two naked souls at war with each other. The plot is as direct and impersonal as a machine, the language as analytically summarized as a scientist's. It looks as though the playwright had become more interested in speculating on the theory of marriage than in the men and women he chose to exemplify his theme.

Reducing his characters to pale shadows of human beings and allowing little space for the development of human traits, O'Neill has made his play less a spectacle of life than a philosophical disquisition. His theme required, I think, a far different sort of treatment. Remember, his man and his woman are bound together by a physical as well as a spiritual bond. Physical love, heaven knows, makes a legitimate and forgivably human appeal in drama, and I see no reason why O'Neill relegated this element not to the background, but completely out of the frame. I have no doubt he felt like Michael, who wanted "to say so much what" he felt, but could "only stutter"—not, of course, precisely "like an idiot," but without heat or light.

What the audience missed in *Welded* was just what I miss in the printed text—the breath of life. I seek men and women and find only a pair of articulated abstractions. I know what O'Neill intends, but he gives me only arguments, explanations, reiterated statements. It is the dramatist's business so to move me—not to persuade or convince or bully—that I shall know and therefore understand something about human beings and life I had not known before, or had only half-felt or perceived. I don't want to admire his logic (at least not until afterward), and as for the technical means that enabled him to achieve the results aimed at, I would have it seem that these never existed.

Welded is a finely conceived but over-intellectualized study, not a well-rounded three-dimensional drama about human beings. It is the skeleton of a possibly fine play. The dramatist was to return later—with too many ideas—to some of the same problems in the extraordinary *Strange Interlude*.

ALL GOD'S CHILLUN GOT WINGS

All God's Chillun Got Wings was written at Provincetown in 1923. No wonder it stirred up trouble when it was first produced at the Provincetown Theatre in May, 1924. Few American playwrights are sufficiently detached to regard intermarriage between whites and blacks in a purely dispassionate mood.

But I think that O'Neill took his situation from life as he found it, because it happened to give him a chance to develop an idea that appealed to him. He was not aroused primarily by the sociological problem of the American Negro any more than Shakespeare was concerned over the civic implications of the quarrel of the Capulets and the Montagues. In each case a playwright found or devised a situation that was full of dramatic possibilities. It is a fact that the marriage of a Negro and a white, at present in the United States, arouses bitterness, dread, fear in the hearts of many whites and Negroes, and between the contracting parties it often precipitates a situation tense with drama. But essentially *All God's Chillun* is a play of love and passion, and not a propaganda piece. There are overtones and suggestions of race memory and fear and hatred, but these are only the accompaniment of the drama. The play is as warmly human as *Welded* is abstract.

The opening scenes show in a seemingly casual way the unself-conscious friendship between black and white youngsters. One of these, an earnest young Negro, has ambitions; he strives to pass his law examinations and makes heroic efforts to overcome what he feels are his racial limitations. He marries a white girl, and for a time the two are happy; but before long they are beset by the problems which arise in this country whenever a black and a white overstep the line which the white man has drawn between his own world and that of the "inferior" Negro. The girl goes crazy and tries to kill her husband, who embodies for her all the innate and unreasoning fears which are her traditional and conventional heritages as a white woman. But she recovers, and asks forgiveness:

> JIM—I wasn't scared of being killed. I was scared of what they'd do to you after.
> ELLA—(*After a pause—like a child*). Will God forgive me, Jim?
> JIM—Maybe He can forgive what you've done to me; and maybe He can forgive what I've done to you; but I don't see how He's going to forgive—Himself.

Here is the lowest point to which the tragedy of this man and woman descends; but it cannot rest there. Tragedy at its purest extends beyond itself when the sufferer is enabled to catch a glimpse of something besides the immediate tragic catastrophe. Though Jim is a "failure," there is in Ella the spark of hope, the symbol of redemption, and just before the play closes Jim "throws himself on his knees and raises his shining eyes, his transfigured face":

> JIM—Forgive me, God—and make me worthy! Now I hear your Voice! . . . Forgive me, God, for blaspheming You! Let this fire of burning suffering purify me of selfishness and make me worthy of the child you send me for the woman you take away!
>
> ELLA—Don't cry, Jim! You mustn't cry! I've got only a little time left and I want to play. Don't be old Uncle Jim now. Be my little boy, Jim. Pretend you're Painty Face and I'm Jim Crow. Come and play!
>
> JIM—Honey, Honey, I'll play right up to the gates of heaven with you!

As a "practical" dramatist O'Neill's error was in making his "nigger" a human being. He even forgot the susceptibilities of those Americans who have laid down the law as to how far a Negro may go in his relations with whites, but recognize no law as to how far a white may go with a Negro. He used a situation so poignant and so tragically beautiful that few otherwise competent critics could see in it a work of art.

Here is a letter O'Neill wrote to a Princeton classmate, printed in *The Fifteen Year Record* of the class of 1910:

"Any appreciation of the worth of that play (*All God's Chillun Got Wings*) is doubly appreciated by me, because of all the prejudiced and unjust knocks it received when it was enjoying such a storm of unwelcome notoriety last winter. It seemed for a time there as if all the feeble-witted both in and out of the K.K.K. were hurling newspaper bricks in my direction—not to speak of the anonymous letters which ranged from those of infuriated Irish Catholics who threatened to pull my ears off as a disgrace to their race and religion, to those of equally infuriated Nordic Kluxers who knew that I had negro blood, or else was a Jewish pervert masquerading under a

Christian name in order to do subversive propaganda for the Pope! This sounds like a burlesque but the letters were more so. And then when the play opened nothing at all happened, not even a senile egg. It was a dreadful anticlimax for all concerned, particularly the critics who seemed to feel cheated that there hadn't been at least one murder that first night. And so on ever since. The whole affair was really a most ludicrous episode—not so ludicrous for me, however, since it put the whole theme of the play on a false basis and thereby threw my whole intent in the production into the discard."

The police, on a technicality, tried to stop the play on the very evening of the opening, by not permitting the children to act in the first scene. But this was read to the audience, and the play went on smoothly. This enraged the police authorities, who not long after stirred up trouble for *Desire Under the Elms.*

A NEW NOTE IN TRAGEDY—*DESIRE UNDER THE ELMS*

Desire Under the Elms, written at Ridgefield during the winter and spring of 1924, marked the highest point so far in O'Neill's development as a tragic writer—the highest point of achievement, but not of aim. In this play he has sounded the depths. He faces life with courage and sanity.

Read what he so admirably stated two years before the play was acted. This was in an interview recorded by Malcolm Mollan, and published in the Philadelphia *Public Ledger* (Jan. 22, 1922):

"Sure I'll write about happiness if I can happen to meet up with that luxury, and find it sufficiently dramatic and in harmony with any deep rhythm in life. But happiness is a word. What does it mean? Exaltation; an intensified feeling of the significant worth of man's being and becoming? Well, if it means that—and not a mere smirking contentment with one's lot—I know there is more of it in one real tragedy than in all the happy-ending plays ever written. It's mere present-day judgment to think of tragedy as unhappy! The Greeks and the Elizabethans knew better. They felt the tremendous lift to it. It roused them spiritually to a deeper understanding of life. Through it they found release from the petty consideration of everyday existence. They saw their lives ennobled by it. A work of art is always happy; all else is unhappy. . . . I don't love life because it's pretty. Prettiness is only clothes-deep. I am a truer lover than that. I love it naked. There is beauty to me even in its ugliness."

In *Desire* he has shown a group of peasants, tenacious in their passion for land, justifying their hardness by their fear of the wrath of God, eager for power, seeking for beauty of a kind, and for sex gratification. These people—unlike people in everyday life!—are cruel and greedy; they talk freely of shameful things fit only to be printed in the Bible.

DESIRE AND THE CENSORS

Desire Under the Elms ran a year in New York, and two road companies did fairly good business with it. During the early part of its run at the Greenwich Village Theatre a New York City official tried his best to close it. He was opposed by a number of persons who believed at least in O'Neill's sincerity, and a play jury system was put into operation to inquire into the morals of such shocking productions as *Desire Under the Elms, They Knew What They Wanted, What Price Glory?*, and *Processional*. The jury could find nothing very subversive in any of them, even in the O'Neill play, which was denounced as the most dangerous of them all.

Ephraim Cabot, a New England farmer who believes that "God is hard" and bases his life on that principle, has just married his third wife, Abbie Putnam, an attractive woman of thirty-five, half his own age. She accepts him in order to provide a home for herself. She finds awaiting her young

Eben, Ephraim's thirty-two-year-old son by his second wife. Believing that the farm belongs rightfully to him, Eben looks upon his new stepmother as a designing and dangerous inter- loper, and he hates her with all the venom of a true son of Ephraim Cabot. Abbie is both clever and sexually attractive, and to keep the farm in her possession she tells her husband that she believes she could conceive a child by him. The old man is delighted and promises that if she should so bless him he will make over his property to the new heir. Abbie then proceeds cold-bloodedly to seduce Eben, but during the process she falls desperately in love with him, as he does with her. A son is born to them, and Ephraim believes it his own. Abbie, for all her cleverness, has aroused in her heart a passion that wrecks all her plans: the lies necessary for carrying out her plot can no longer be concealed, and Eben tells every- thing to his father. Ephraim then destroys the last vestige of Eben's illusion by telling him what was, not long since, the literal truth: that Abbie has pretended to love him only in order to make sure of the property. The young man, in a fury of rage and disappointment, decides to leave home at once, to Abbie's utter despair. The irony of the situation is not clear to her; she is so deeply attached to Eben that she cannot con- vince him that though in the beginning she did make love to him for an ulterior purpose, she is now completely mastered by her passion. She frantically tells him that she loves him for his own sake, but he will not listen. She must now prove at any cost that she is sincere. She therefore strangles the child. Eben is at last convinced of her love for him, but is so horri- fied at her act that he runs off at once and tells the police.

The last scene finds the lovers once more in each other's arms. Eben confesses that he is an accomplice and he is ready to pay the penalty with Abbie. They are taken off by the sheriff and his men, happy and exultant. They have drunk deep of life and passion, and they have no regrets. They have passed out of the realm where tragedy—as ordinarily under- stood—can touch them. Of "sin" they have no consciousness:

victims of puritanical repressions, of unrestrained passion and of the mighty current of life, they have fashioned their romance apart from the sordidness of their surroundings. Though they have lived among those whose religion is hateful, they have broken through into the light of day. There among the rocks and the hard soil where they yearned for beauty, they have at last found it.

The framework of this tragedy is rather elaborate; two almost superfluous scenes are introduced at first in order to show Eben's older half-brothers leaving the farm for California (the time is 1850). But the unity of the play lies in the character of Abbie. In arousing the repressed passion of Eben she has forgotten, or perhaps she had never known, that the sex instinct cannot easily be controlled; she has depended on her own craftiness to see her machinations through in cold blood to the end. Then suddenly she finds herself caught in her own trap.

It is in the scenes where Abbie begins to realize that she has precipitated a power she cannot cope with that O'Neill proves himself a master. There is little trace here of "theater": a trick would spoil everything. He must push on relentlessly to his conclusion. What does Abbie do? She cannot give Eben up, and she cannot remain with Ephraim. She has to show, by violent means, that she cares nothing for the property. One thing stands between them: the child. She therefore kills him.

Now I do not believe that Abbie would deliberately murder her baby. I believe she would have killed Ephraim, and I think that that is what she ought to have done in the play. But the point cannot be decided by reference to any canon of criticism.

The murder is not convincing. I think it is a mistake, yet it does not seriously affect the play. The rest follows inevitably: as in All God's Chillun, the dawn breaks on the figures of a man and a woman calmly facing whatever the day shall bring them. "Life doesn't end. One experience is but the birth of another." Even death itself.

TRANSITION EXPERIMENTS AND *THE FOUNTAIN*

The Fountain was written at Provincetown in 1921 and 1922.
It was first acquired by Arthur Hopkins, and then by the
Theater Guild, but it was ultimately produced by Jones,
Macgowan and O'Neill at the Greenwich Village Theatre in
1925. It ran there for just two weeks and was pretty generally
condemned by the press and the few audiences that went to
see it. On the whole, the play in production seemed rather
dull, which was in a way due to the long waits between the
scenes; partly the fault of the actors, most of whom had not
been trained for romantic acting; and partly that of the playwright. This play, as conventional in form as *Cyrano de
Bergerac,* came as a surprise to nearly everyone who knew the
work of O'Neill; actually it shows only another aspect of
his outlook on life. It has to do with the almost wholly imaginary story of the quest for the Fountain of Youth by Juan
Ponce de Leon and his final realization that such ventures are
and must be doomed to failure when rationally or materialis-
tically conceived, though they become glorious events when
identified with the quest for life, love and beauty. "One must
accept," says Juan, "absorb, give back, become oneself a
symbol. . . . Juan Ponce de Leon is past! He is resolved into
the thousand moods of beauty that make up happiness—color
of that sunset, of tomorrow's dawn, breath of the great Trade
Wind—sunlight on the grass, an insect's song, the rustle of
leaves, an ant's ambitions. I shall know eternal becoming—
eternal youth!"

The chant that runs through the play is a lyrical comment
on the theme:

> Love is a flower
> Forever blooming,
> Beauty a fountain
> Forever flowing
> Upward into the source of sunshine,

Upward into the azure heaven;
One with God but
Ever returning
To kiss the earth that the flower may live.

As poetry these lines are not distinguished, but when chanted in a theater they help to establish a poetic mood.

The Fountain is, in conception, a dramatic poem of exaltation—the reflection of the poet's never-ending aspiration.

Juan seeks the actual Fountain of Youth and his life is dedicated to the task of finding it; unscrupulous and cruel, he follows a rainbow until the pursuit becomes a mania. Yet no dreamer finds what he sets out to attain, though some are rewarded in discovering something else and abandoning as worthless what they once desired. Through tragedy they may learn the lesson of life, divining at last that the effort is worth while in itself. Juan cannot become young again, but he does learn that "there is no gold but love."

O'Neill's note on the program is instructive and amusing:

"The idea," he says, "of writing *The Fountain* came on finally from my interest in the recurrence in folklore of the beautiful legend of a healing spring of eternal youth. The play is only incidentally concerned with the Era of Discovery in America. It has sought merely to express the urging spirit of that period without pretending to any too educational accuracy in the matter of dates and facts in general. The characters, with the exception of Columbus, are fictitious. Juan Ponce de Leon, in so far as I've been able to make him a human being, is wholly imaginary. I have simply filled in the bare outline of his career, as briefly reported in the Who's Who of the histories, with a conception of what could have been the truth behind his 'life-sketch' if he had been the man it was romantically—and religiously—moving to me to believe he might have been! Therefore, I wish to take solemn oath right here and now that *The Fountain* is not morbid realism."

In spite of its conception and the beauty of certain scenes, *The Fountain* is not a spontaneous or very moving work. O'Neill had adopted a form not altogether in harmony with his temperament. To be entirely successful, a play of this kind must be written somewhat naïvely, with more passion than reflection: and it should master the poet. The trouble here is that the poet knew the form so well that he mastered *it*. Then there is the matter of language. There are scenes toward the end that cry aloud not for fine writing or mere literature but for poetry, formal verse. The poetic urge, the heat of the poet's passion, seems striving to burst the bonds of prose, demanding the formal freedom of inspired verse. And no matter how hard he tried, O'Neill had not yet been able to acquire a mastery of felicitous language. There is something labored in his purple patches. J. Brooks Atkinson, in the *Times* of Dec. 20, 1925, hit the nail on the head when he wrote that the play "rarely stirs the emotions or gives spur to the imagination. . . . The austere self-criticism that prompted Mr. O'Neill to destroy sixteen of his dramas as unworthy of production has in this instance indulged him too freely."

In John Mason Brown's *Letters From Greenroom Ghosts* (1934), there is an imaginary letter to O'Neill from Christopher Marlowe. The entire letter, incidentally, offers some of the best criticism yet written on O'Neill. I quote one sentence here because it expresses with admirable clarity what is chiefly wrong with *The Fountain*. The ghost of Marlowe speaks: "The dramas you have begotten do not flash with the blinding sunlight of naked swords as did my blood-drenched chronicles."

THE ANCIENT MARINER

The Ancient Mariner, "a Dramatic Arrangement of Coleridge's Poem," was produced in 1924 at the Provincetown Playhouse. Here for the first time O'Neill used masks. In the

Provincetown Playbill James Light, one of the producers, writes: "We are using masks in *The Ancient Mariner* for this reason: that we wish to project certain dramatic motifs through that spiritual atmosphere which the mask peculiarly gives. . . . We are trying to use it to show the eyes of tragedy and the face of exaltation."

The play was somewhat dull in production. It was not successful and it has never been published.

In O'Neill's next play the mask becomes an important technical factor.

SYMBOLISM AND *THE GREAT GOD BROWN*

The Great God Brown, written in Bermuda in 1925, was produced (partly at the author's own expense, after Otto Kahn had declined to back it) at the Greenwich Village Theatre in January, 1926. This play, so far as its conception is concerned, is one of the most subtle and effective things O'Neill has ever written. In it he has sought to exhibit, in a vibrant lyrical style, man's aspirations; it is a dramatic pæan to man's struggle to identify himself with nature. The tone throughout is mystically ecstatic. Man's way is seen here winding through the vale of tragedy, but it emerges triumphant.

In order to dispense with some otherwise necessary explanation the dramatist has devised masks for nearly all his characters. "So far as I know," says Kenneth Macgowan in the program notes, "O'Neill's play is the first in which masks have ever been used to dramatize changes and conflicts in character." He uses them as a "means of dramatizing a transfer of personality from one man to another."

In his *Memoranda on Masks* (*American Spectator,* Nov. 1932) O'Neill writes that "for certain types of plays, especially for the new modern play, the use of masks will be discovered to be the freest solution of the modern dramatist's problem as to how . . . he can express those profound hidden conflicts of the mind which the probings of psychology continue to disclose to us . . . What, at bottom, is the new psychological insight into human cause and effect but a study in masks, an exercise in unmasking?"

The Great God Brown requires explanation, and this the author himself furnished in a letter to the papers. I reprint all of it here, as printed in the New York *Evening Post*, Feb. 13, 1926:

> I realize that when a playwright takes to explaining he thereby automatically places himself "in the dock." But where an open-faced avowal by the play itself of the abstract theme underlying it is made impossible by the very nature of that hidden theme, then perhaps it is justifiable for the author to confess the mystical pattern which manifests itself as an overtone in *The Great God Brown,* dimly behind and beyond the words and actions of the characters.
>
> I had hoped the names chosen for my people would give a strong hint of this. (An old scheme, admitted—Shakespeare and multitudes since.) Dion Anthony—Dionysus and St. Anthony—the creative pagan acceptance of life, fighting eternal war with the masochistic, life-denying spirit of Christianity as represented by St. Anthony—the whole struggle resulting in this modern day in mutual exhaustion—creative joy in life for life's sake frustrated, rendered abortive, distorted by morality from Pan into Satan, into a Mephistopheles mocking himself in order to feel alive; Christianity, once heroic in martyrs for its intense faith now pleading weakly for intense belief in anything, even Godhead itself. (In the play it is Cybele, the pagan Earth Mother, who makes the assertion with authority: "Our Father, Who Art!" to the dying Brown, as it is she who tries to inspire Dion Anthony with her certainty in life for its own sake.)
>
> Margaret is my image of the modern direct descendant of the Marguerite of Faust—the eternal girl-woman with a virtuous simplicity of instinct, properly oblivious to everything but the means to her end of maintaining the race.
>
> Cybel is an incarnation of Cybele, the Earth Mother doomed to segregation as a pariah in a world of unnatural laws, but

patronized by her segregators, who are thus themselves the first victims of their laws.

Brown is the visionless demi-god of our new materialistic myth—a Success—building his life of exterior things, inwardly empty and resourceless, an uncreative creature of superficial preordained social grooves, a by-product forced aside into slack waters by the deep main current of life-desire.

Dion's mask of Pan which he puts on as a boy is not only a defense against the world for the supersensitive painter-poet underneath it, but also an integral part of his character as the artist. The world is not only blind to the man beneath, but it also sneers at and condemns the Pan-mask it sees. After that Dion's inner self retrogresses along the line of Christian resignation until it partakes of the nature of the Saint while at the same time the outer Pan is slowly transformed by his struggle with reality into Mephistopheles. It is as Mephistopheles he falls stricken at Brown's feet after having condemned Brown to destruction by willing him his mask, but, this mask falling off as he dies, it is the Saint who kisses Brown's feet in abject contrition and pleads as a little boy to a big brother to tell him a prayer.

Brown has always envied the creative life force in Dion— what he himself lacks. When he steals Dion's mask of Mephistopheles he thinks he is gaining the power to live creatively, while in reality he is only stealing that creative power made self-destructive by complete frustration. This devil of mocking doubt makes short work of him. It enters him, rending him apart, torturing and transfiguring him until he is even forced to wear a mask of his Success, William A. Brown, before the world, as well as Dion's mask toward wife and children. Thus Billy Brown becomes not himself to anyone. And thus he partakes of Dion's anguish—more poignantly, for Dion has the Mother, Cybele—and in the end out of this anguish his soul is born, a tortured Christian soul such as the dying Dion's, begging for belief, and at the last finding it on the lips of Cybel.

And now for an explanation regarding this explanation. It was far from my idea in writing *Brown* that this background pattern of conflicting tides in the soul of Man should ever overshadow and thus throw out of proportion the living drama of the recognizable human beings, Dion, Brown, Margaret and Cybel. I meant it always to be mystically within and behind them, giving them a significance beyond themselves, forcing itself through them to expression in mysterious words, symbols, actions they do not themselves comprehend. And that is as clearly as I wish an audience to comprehend it. It is Mystery— the mystery any one man or woman can feel but not understand as the meaning of any event—or accident—in any life on earth. And it is this mystery I want to realize in the theater. The solution, if there ever be any, will probably have to be produced in a test tube and turn out to be discouragingly undramatic.

I'm afraid this explanation calls for further explanation, and I think I have it, almost verbatim from the dramatist himself. It does not, of course, clarify the whole statement, but it throws a sidelight upon it. Before the play was put on he asked what chance I thought it had in the theater, and I said I would give it about two weeks, long enough for the O'Neill fans to take a look at it.

"You may be right," he answered, "but I somehow feel there's enough in it to get over to unsophisticated audiences. In one sense *Brown* is a mystery play, only instead of dealing with crooks and police it's about the mystery of personality and life. I shouldn't be surprised if it interested people who won't bother too much over every shade of meaning, but follow it as they follow any story. They needn't understand with their minds, they can just watch and feel."

And O'Neill was right, for the play ran nearly a year.

I don't know whether O'Neill has heard the story about the two shop-girls who went to see it when it moved uptown? It shows the attitude of most of the audiences who continued to patronize it during its long run. After the third act one of them turned to the other. "Gee, it's awful artistic, ain't it?" she said. "Yes," was the answer, "but it's good all the same."

The Great God Brown, as I have said, is one of the subtlest of all O'Neill's plays; beyond a doubt it is fuller than any other of the poet's sense of the rhythm and harmony and multifariousness of life. The language expresses—and where it doesn't express it hints at—shades of half-realized meanings that are difficult to shape into phrases and sentences, but on the whole the style is better fitted to the subject than in some of the later plays.

Yet it is not as technically perfect as *Desire Under the Elms* nor even as *The Hairy Ape*: it aims too high, it puts a burden upon the director and the actor that neither has successfully borne. I believe that in the theater all but the play itself should be no more than a humble adjunct to the dramatic poet, and that no production can illuminate or clarify the inner significance of any imaginative work, though it may add other elements, perhaps even a surpassing beauty quite apart from what is in the text itself. Though *The Great God Brown* was directed and played with skill and understanding, there was too much self-consciousness and "pointing." To produce a play of this sort we must have simplicity of mind and an extreme plasticity of emotion, in order that the purely theatrical qualities of the show, as show, shall stand out above every shade of individual interpretation on the part of actor or director. I feel that the director and players were too familiar with the author's intentions, instead of playing the thing straight ahead and leaving to O'Neill the task of putting these intentions across.

MARCO MILLIONS

IN MARCH, 1925, O'Neill finished work on *Marco Millions*. But he had been busy with it for a long time before. I am told that the idea came to him before he began writing *The Fountain*, in 1921. It had evidently been two plays, or one play in two parts not long before the final script was ready, intended for production on successive evenings, for in a letter he says that he decided to "rewrite and condense the two nights into one long night." The play had been acquired some time before March, 1925, by David Belasco, but after a year's delay Belasco still hesitated to produce it, claiming that it would cost too much money. So the script went the rounds again. Gilbert Miller and Arthur Hopkins both turned it down, and O'Neill suggested to Nathan, who was trying to interest managers, that Ames, Dillingham, Gest and Walter Hampden might want to see it. Ames seems to have read the play and refused it, and there was talk later of Horace Liver-right raising the necessary money. In September, 1926, O'Neill wrote Nathan that the Theatre Guild's committee "has definitely decided they want the play—but they could not do it for over a year."

Contracts were at last signed with the Guild, though *Marco* was not produced until 1928.

In 1926 I read the script. Though it was the condensed version I saw, it was longer by at least two scenes than the one ultimately acted. I had gone through it quickly and in returning it to O'Neill I told him I thought it was a gorgeous and beautiful comedy. And so it was, but in reading it rapidly I had not calculated that what could be read in two minutes might, because of the elaborate stage business described in the text, require five in the acting.

As to the origin of *Marco*, we know that the idea was in O'Neill's mind for years, but what may have put the sting into its bitterest scenes is an incident reported by George Jean Nathan in *The American Mercury* in 1927:

"When Mr. [Otto] Kahn turned his haughty critical shoulder upon this play (the *Great God Brown*) he asked O'Neill why he didn't give up writing such things and turn his hand instead to something which he, Kahn, might be proud to endorse. And what was this something? O'Neill timidly wished to know. A play apotheosizing American big business and the American business man—a man like Mr. Kahn, for example, came the reply. O'Neill coughed and bowed himself from the great presence. His answer was to write *Marco Millions,* the sourest and most magnificent poke in the jaw that American big business and the American business man have ever got."

To this O'Neill added, when I saw him a year before Nathan wrote his squib, that Kahn had offered to let him in at a private directors' meeting in Wall Street. "A lot I'd have learned there!" he snorted. "Can you imagine those fellows exposing their big schemes in the presence of a suspicious-looking outsider?"

In all fairness to Mr. Kahn I must say it did not seem to be his idea that O'Neill should glorify Big Business, but only write about it. Maybe I am mistaken, though. I can't imagine that Kahn would be so stupid as to invite O'Neill, of all men, to apotheosize Business; but on the other hand if he was, that would account for his seeing nothing in *The Great God Brown* and *Marco Millions.*

O'Neill's Foreword to *Marco* is worth looking at:

"This play," he writes, "is an attempt to render poetic justice to one long famous as a traveler, unjustly world-renowned as a liar, but sadly unrecognized by posterity in his true eminence as a man and a citizen—Marco Polo of Venice. The failure to appraise Polo at a fair valuation is his own fault. He dictated the book of his travels but left the traveler out. He was no author. He stuck to a recital of what he considered facts and the world called him a liar for his pains. Even in his native Venice he was scoffingly nicknamed 'the millionaire,' or 'Marco Millions.' They could not take seriously his impressive statistics about the 'millions' of this and the 'millions' of that in the East. Polo, the man of brass tacks, became celebrated as an extravagant romancer and ever since has traveled down the prejudiced centuries, a prophet without honor, or even notoriety, save in false whiskers. This has moved me to an indignant crusade between the lines of his book, the bars of his prison, in order to whitewash the good soul of that maligned Venetian."

Marco Millions is one of the less ambitious works of our playwright. I make this statement after some reflection, a re-reading of the text, and watching a beautiful production of it by the Theatre Guild. My first enthusiasm was genuine, but in the script there was no need to wait for scene changes nor to sit in a theater where flesh-and-blood actors were under the necessity of acting out in too great detail each bit of fleeting dialogue, emphasizing what should have been compressed or—occasionally—omitted.

The play is a romantic satire on Occidental hard-headedness set against a colorful background of medieval Oriental civilization. In ten scenes Marco Polo is shown pursuing his career from boyhood to early middle age, and finally to Success. He begins as a nice young man and ends up a Babbitt, minus Babbitt's idealism. The beauty and romance, the serenity and wisdom of an age-old culture, mean nothing to him. The loveliness of a way of life so different from what he has known, and what he desires, is utterly wasted on him. His sojourn in the land of Kublai Khan is merely an opportunity for amassing a fortune.

Here is a brilliant though not a new idea for a delightful comedy, but the idea alone is not enough to fill so many scenes and a long evening in the playhouse.

The Guild did nobly by *Marco Millions*. The settings and costumes were entrancing. Of one thing only I must complain: the waits between scenes.

Stretched out to two and a half hours *Marco* seemed rather thin. I believe that if it had been reduced to five or six scenes, acted on a revolving stage without intermission and turned into a dramatic ballet with dancing, music, pantomime and dialogue, it would have been a perfect thing of its kind.

Here again I repeat that in some of his later plays the dramatist shows a growing tendency to write "fine" speeches and embroider purple patches. *The Fountain* had many of them, and *The Great God Brown* a few. I am not here referring to the dialogue in general, but to the rhetorical effusions of Ponce de Leon and Kublai and Dion. I can't rid myself of the impression that O'Neill was striving for effects. His gift for poetry lies not in written speeches, but in his conceptions, in scenes and situations, and occasionally in separate lines that illuminate not by their intrinsic verbal values but by their implications.

STRANGE INTERLUDE

WHEN I saw O'Neill in June, 1926, he told me about one of the new plays he was working on. The idea sounded preposterous: there were to be nine acts, and all the characters were to speak their thoughts aloud, with no regard for the ordinary conventions of the theater or of normal social intercourse.

"And why not?" he asked. "Everything is a matter of convention. If we accept one, why not another, so long as it does what it's intended to do? My people speak aloud what they think and what the others aren't supposed to hear. They talk in prose, realistic or otherwise—blank verse or hexameter or rhymed couplets." Then he went on to outline the story. The actual writing of *Strange Interlude* was done in Bermuda and Maine in 1926 and 1927.

The Theatre Guild contracted for the play, and early in 1928 it was produced. The Guild people have a way of doing things well. We know from the published letters of O'Neill that the Guild had turned down *The Fountain* when the prestige of a production by them would have helped immensely, and the royalties have eked out an income that was none too large; and there had been misunderstandings about other early MSS. But to the Guild O'Neill owes adequate, careful, and on occasion superb productions, and it is likely that if that group had not produced *Strange Interlude* and *Dynamo*, he might have had a hard time in those years finding other producers willing or able to take chances on them.

Let me begin my remarks on *Strange Interlude* by saying that the producers and director spared no pains or expense in doing ample justice to the drama. There have been few plays that required more tact and skill and imagination than this ambitious and subtle play in nine acts. Philip Moeller never directed anything that called for greater intelligence and a more sympathetic understanding. He brought into relief as much as was possible in a work that has so little that is conventionally theatrical. There is not much of that "pointing," straining after effect, that has marred certain other Guild productions.

Strange Interlude is many things, almost as many things as it has been called. The first point to make is that from 5:30 P.M. until after eleven, except for eighty minutes' intermission for supper, it holds the audience. Yet not primarily by means of theatrical trickery. It is not the story, which could easily have been condensed into three acts; it is not the strangeness of the asides and monologues (that novelty wears off in a few minutes); it is no more nor less than the triumph of O'Neill's art, his amazing gift for understanding and laying bare some of the complexities of the human mind and heart. He was clearly unwilling to make use of the traditional dramatic form which, in its latest manifestations, does not admit the aside and the soliloquy, and refuses to allow the dramatist much more than two or two and a quarter hours' time.

He had therefore, with a characteristic disregard of current fashions, elaborated what might otherwise have been a commonplace plot into nine acts, with a total playing time almost twice as long as what we are used to. There is more to hold the attention in *Strange Interlude* than there is in *Parsifal*. There is less "literature" but far more drama than there is in *Faust*. *Strange Interlude* carries four characters through their chief emotional crises during twenty-seven or -eight years. Nina Leeds, daughter of a college professor, loses her fiancé shortly after he goes to war to be an aviator. Her puritanical father has prevented the consummation of their union, which precipitates her decision to leave home. At first she becomes a nurse, then she seeks other outlets for her more or less imperfectly adjusted desires and aspirations. As she enters the main action of the play she has already begun to take on the appearance and characteristics of woman—with a capital W—to symbolize the Earth Spirit; she is a close relation of Cybel in *The Great God Brown;* she is mother, wife, mistress, adultress, materialist, idealist. Into her life are woven strands from the lives of many men: of Gordon (a romantic memory and an ideal); of the patient mother-ridden Charles Marsden; of Sam, her husband; of Edmund Darrell, her lover; and later of her son Gordon. For this woman no one man is enough. This epic creature, endowed with an inordinate thirst for life, takes on the proportions of a superwoman. With dreams that can never quite be fulfilled, held in check by inhibitions, forced onward by appetites, she is the incarnation of vitality, a creature that is driven to meddle in the lives of others in order that her own life may be filled to overflowing. No one is a match for her; nothing arrests her progress, nothing but old age. At last she is defeated by time and by that very spirit of youth (in the person of her son) that urged her on to rebel when she was young. The boy Gordon and the girl he is determined to marry leave her, even as she had left her helpless father.

This, essentially, is the "story" of *Strange Interlude*. There are several plot incidents, absorbing in themselves, but introduced principally to throw the character of Nina into sharp relief. I see in the play no "moral," no "intention," indeed very little of any definite philosophy. This in spite of what O'Neill and some of his interpreters have said on the subject. It was O'Neill's aim to expose imaginatively a chain of events in which a few people exhibit to us their thoughts and motives over a long period of years. Life offers us problems, joys, tragedies; it seems to take shape occasionally as a thing of beauty, but oftener as a senseless and cruel joke; yet it is an exciting process, a great adventure. The puppets we call ourselves are momentarily self-important with their little schemes for cheating death and avoiding unhappiness, but ultimately they lose bit by bit their desires and the fierce impulses of youth, declining slowly into a sunset period where peace alone seems worth having. Thus Nina seems to outgrow and cast off her sex, to embody and to be identified with the life instinct. Because she is conceived by the dramatist as a woman, each situation in her life is symbolized by a man, possessing something that she needs, has needed, or will need at last. In the case of Marsden we see her carefully appraising him in the first act and marking him out for use at some future time; at the end of the ninth act, when everything else has gone, she falls into his protecting arms, there to pass peacefully the remaining days of her life.

I have not yet touched on the essential element in *Strange Interlude*—the thing that makes it, with all its faults, a masterly creation. This is no more nor less than the dramatist's divination and dramatization of the motives of his people. As I have said, he could easily have told his story in three acts, but he extended it to nine in order that he might not have to say, "If I had had time, I might have told you everything essential about these people." He did have time, because he took it; he probably took a little too much time, not his own, but ours; there are places where he has insisted on making his characters explain to us what has already been clearly shown.

We are almost immediately let into the secrets of these characters: they tell us a great deal of what they think and feel. Not everything, of course, for that would be impossible and not at all necessary, but enough for the purpose at hand. The thoughts expressed aloud cannot at best constitute more than a fraction of those half-thoughts, hints and shadowings that haunt the subconscious mind, but they are enough for O'Neill. Shakespeare did much the same thing, and so did Goethe. O'Neill has tried to go a little farther, and has used the device somewhat more realistically. If he had been a Shakespeare or a Goethe he could have succeeded where they did, and with less ado. Simple and crude as it is, the device he uses is occasionally very effective. That is why there is no surprise in the ordinary sense; no suspense, and no curiosity of the sort aroused in conventional fiction. O'Neill knows that *Strange Interlude* is heavy with suspense, and for this reason he throws overboard most of the devices by which dramatists usually create it. He never releases the tension in his pursuit of the motives of human activity; this is his aim throughout. Like a surgeon he cuts deep, knowing always just what he is after.

While he has succeeded in showing a series of events each of which throws into relief some basic characteristic of one or more persons; and while he has conceived largely and written nobly, I feel that *Strange Interlude* is not the perfect work it might have been. For one thing, the shade of Strindberg hovers too close over it all: there is something strained, a bit diagrammatic and intellectualized in the character of Nina. She is rather too special—too much the female of the species. Woman as a beast of prey is Strindberg's invention, and I don't think O'Neill's vision of the world is as narrow and warped as that of the Swedish poet.

Technically, what of the asides and the nine acts? Is it always necessary in a play to express aloud what one thinks and feels? Cannot the actor occasionally show it? I believe that perhaps half of all the words not intended to be heard by the other characters might have been omitted without the loss of anything essential. O'Neill has overworked his device.

Finally, there is something lacking in the last three acts. They are somewhat repetitious, and might well have been condensed into one.

In these acts we notice again the dramatist's tendency to get lost in the mazes of his own rhetoric, not because he is trying merely to write for the sake of writing, but because he insists on exploring to the utmost the darkest corners of the mind and heart. In becoming familiar with the shape and color of words every writer has to guard against the temptation to create "mere" literature, or what looks like it, for he too often becomes the slave, as Stevenson and Wilde did, of the thing he thinks he has conquered. Throughout *Strange Interlude*, particularly in the asides, there are some lapses into "fine" writing. Of course, I am not insisting that one's thoughts ought not to be well expressed, but good expression does not of course mean "fine" writing, and some of O'Neill's fine writing is not good expression. In his attempt to avoid the banalities of surface realism he sometimes falls into another sort of error.

LAZARUS LAUGHED

ALONE of all the O'Neill plays completed and intended for the stage since his apprentice days, *Lazarus Laughed* has not yet been professionally acted, nor has there been a single performance of any kind in New York City.

In April 1928 it was first produced under the direction of Gilmor Brown, at the Pasadena Community Playhouse, by a company of nonprofessional players.

Shortly after the MS. was finished (in 1926) O'Neill told me he thought it was the "most successful thing I ever did. I think I've got it just right. It *is*, from my viewpoint. It's in seven scenes, and all the characters wear masks. And here I've used them right. In *Brown* I couldn't know beforehand how the scheme would work out. They were too realistic there, and sitting way back in the theater you couldn't be sure if the actors had on masks or not. I should have had them twice as large—and conventionalized them, so the audience could get the idea at once. In *Lazarus* I believe I've managed the problem of big crowds better than crowds are usually worked in plays. It's never quite right. My Jews all wear Jewish masks, and it's the same with the Greeks and Romans. I think I've suggested the presence and characteristics of mobs (by means of masks) without having to bring in a lot of supers. I also have a chorus of seven, who chant together, emphasizing and 'pointing' the action throughout. Then there are other new stunts. I've worked out every detail of the setting and action, even the lighting. Incidentally, I've done the same thing with all my plays, only (with a smile) I didn't get credit for it. I guess I ought to have that mentioned on the programs!"

O'Neill calls his work a "Play for an Imaginative Theater," but he might more appropriately have said an Imaginary Theater. There is so much in *Lazarus* that can only be blunted and vulgarized by taking it into the playhouse, that he ought to be content to leave it, as Hardy left *The Dynasts,* for production in the "theater of the mind."

Lazarus Laughed is first of all the exposition of a philosophy of life and death. Here we are concerned more with the idea than with the characters. Lazarus has risen from the tomb and after Jesus departed he began to laugh "softly like a man in love with God," walking abroad from that time on, preaching his doctrine that "Death is the fear between." The chorus chant

> Laugh! Laugh!
> There is only life!
> There is only laughter!
> Fear is no more!
> Death is dead!

Fortified by his faith, Lazarus fears nothing as he tests its validity by setting himself against those who fear life in fearing death. He even attempts to convert the Emperor Tiberius. The materialistic philosophy of the Roman cannot resist the ecstatic Lazarus, and even though Tiberius orders him killed, the prophet of eternal life is triumphant. At the end Caligula the scoffer, the degenerate heir of Tiberius, is almost won over to the new faith, and as the curtain falls he cries out "Fool! Madman! Forgive me, Lazarus!"

Lazarus Laughed is a hymn to life, a cry of triumph shouted in the faces of those Christians who look upon existence as a vale of tears, the petty egotists who expect an everlasting happiness in heaven because they lack the courage to be content on earth. O'Neill's conception of immortality, though not new, is a happy and courageous one. He resents the impudent insult to "life's nobility which gibbers 'I, this Jew, this Roman . . . must survive in my pettiness forever!'" Into the mouth of Lazarus, who possesses a Will to Live not for his own sake but for all men, he has put words that express the essence of this philosophy: "Believe! What if you are a man and men are despicable? Men are also unimportant! Men pass! Like rain into the sea! The sea remains! Man remains! Man slowly arises from the past of the race of men that was his tomb of death! For Man death is not! Man, Son of God's Laughter, *is!*"

It will be remembered that at the end of *Desire Under the Elms* a man and a woman sit silently waiting for their punishment, yet there was no note of impending doom, only a moment of peace and serenity. For the first time the victims of fate in an O'Neill play had faced death not as failure, but as ultimate justification—the crowning moment that fulfilled for them the experience through which they have lived: the beauty of the passion of Abbie and Eben transcended the "tragedy" of their crime and punishment. In *Marco Millions* the idealistic boy was turned into a hard-headed man of commerce who saw nothing of the beauty of Kukachin; yet her loveliness persisted, even after death. In *Strange Interlude*, too, there is a serenity that emerges not out of the denial of life but from a mighty affirmation of it, when Nina says to Charlie, "Yes, our lives are merely strange dark interludes in the electrical display of God the Father!"

Of the validity of O'Neill's philosophy in *Lazarus Laughed* there is no need to speak at length. Personally, it appeals to me, and that is why the play written to propound it seems a little better in my eyes than it really is. But I object first of all to the dramatist's playing the role of thinker and prophet; I object to the artist's putting his talent at the disposal of the propagandist. Like most converts to a new idea, O'Neill is not content to state, he must reiterate and hammer away until the densest listener understands what he is driving at. Half the choruses of *Lazarus* should be cut, and a great many of Lazarus' lines; there is little development in the play, which is over-written; in spots it is even somewhat bombastic. There is of course a somber beauty in the conception and there are passages of lyrical loveliness, but these are not enough.

There is no reason why O'Neill should not try to portray characters in the throes of mental and spiritual torture, but the moment he himself tries to solve the riddle of the universe he is lost. It is my opinion that in his impatience to widen the scope of the theater he has too quickly passed from what he considers the superficialities of Realism into the rarefied regions of the abstract.

If O'Neill were a genuinely original thinker or even a brilliant spokesman for the ideas of a brilliant thinker, we might argue as to whether we should be the losers if he were to give up writing plays altogether, but his ideas as contributions to contemporary thought are negligible.

I demand of no artist that he explain or expound life, so long as he portrays it with truth and passion. By means of these he is enabled to give us in terms different from the terms of the philosopher his own implicit judgment on the world and all that dwell therein. Leonardo painted his *Mona Lisa* and when he laid down the brush for the last time his job was done. He left it to others to elaborate upon its implications. What Pater wrote about the picture can never affect the picture itself.

DYNAMO

Dynamo, written in France in 1928, was produced by the Theatre Guild in February, 1929. In an article that appeared shortly before the opening Kenneth Macgowan described its origin. One day O'Neill stood watching a dynamo at a plant near Ridgefield, Connecticut, where electricity is generated from the waters of New England rivers. There was something in the machine that suggested a new god, just as the stone images of the past symbolized the old gods. The great hydro-electric generator in the play "is huge and black, with something of a great massive ebony idol about it, the 'exciter' set on the main structure like a round head with oblong eyes above the squat torso."

That *Dynamo* ought not to be regarded entirely as an independent work is clear from Macgowan's words. "In essence," he writes, "it is a clearing ground for the erection of other structures." It may be, he continues, the "beginning of a bridge between emotional reality and lyric faith."

> The dramatist himself wrote that the play is a "symbolical and factual biography of what is happening in a large section of the American (and not only American) soul right now. It is really the first play of a trilogy that will dig at the roots of the sickness of today as I feel it—the death of an old God and the failure of science and materialism to give any satisfying new one for the surviving primitive religious instinct to find a meaning for life in, and to comfort its fears of death with. It seems to me that anyone trying to do big work nowadays must have this big subject behind all the little subjects of his plays or novels, or he is simply scribbling around on the surface of things and has no more real status than a parlor entertainer. . . . The other two plays will be *Without Ending of Days* and *It Cannot Be Mad*."

There was an ominous note in all this: O'Neill seemed to be worrying too much about God and his own soul. I believe he was doing too much of his own private thinking aloud, playing an autobiographical *Strange Interlude* with long asides that ought to have been ruthlessly cut. Perhaps he hadn't the patience to let his philosophy of life mature, but must out with it incontinently?

To return to *Dynamo*. It was to have been only the beginning, the first chapter, a fragment, and whatever judgment we passed on it should be modified by the plays that were to follow. *Dynamo* is the tragedy of a young man who loses faith in the "old God of dogma, imagines that he recovers it in the sleek image of an electric dynamo and soon finds himself worshipping it with the same Calvinistic vehemence, superstition and madness. Having violated the vow of chastity made in pious devotion to the new electric god, he casts himself into the dynamo in a graphic final scene." (Brooks Atkinson in the New York *Times*, Feb. 12, 1929).

The story of Reuben Light and his rapid conversions from Fundamentalism to Atheism, and from Atheism to the worship of science, is told with some skill and few digressions. The first two acts are laid successively in each of four rooms of the adjacent homes of the Fundamentalist and the Atheist. We see into these houses that stand stripped of their walls, looking like skeletons of wooden framework, hideous and bare. The young man falls in love with Ada Fife of the Atheist family, and most of the action centers round the boy and the girl. The last act is laid inside the huge power plant.

Up to the last part of the final act, O'Neill carries through a straightforward plot, and then he evidently plants a situation as an emplacement for the next play. I am not certain just why Reuben considers Ada a necessary obstacle in the way of embracing a new religion, or why the dynamo so jealously prevents his union with the girl. Without sufficient reason, it seems to me, Reuben shoots and kills Ada. Then he prays to the dynamo: "O Dynamo, God of Electricity, which gives life to all things, hear my prayer! Receive me into the Great Current of Your Eternal Life. Bless me with Your secret so that I can save men from sin and sorrow and death! Grant me the miracle of Your love." At the end he "throws his arms over the head of the dynamo; his hands grasp the carbon brushes of the exciter. In a flash all the lights in the plant dim down until they are almost out and the noise of the dynamo dies until it is the faintest hum. Simultaneously his voice rises in a sobbing cry of pain."

Dynamo pointed to a sequel, but no matter what the next play was to have been, the fact remains that *Dynamo* was released to the public as one play alone. Fortunately, I think, O'Neill decided not to complete the two plays that were, with *Dynamo*, to have formed a trilogy. *Dynamo* may be looked upon in two entirely different ways. In intention it is Promethean, a challenge to our civilization, an attempt to synthesize in the form of a modern morality play some of the most baffling intellectual and theological problems of our time. Potentially, it is charged with poetry and the fire of youthful imagination. Judged as it must finally be judged, as a work of art, it fails because it remains at best little more than the skeleton of a magnificent effort, like the bare outlines of the two houses in the stage setting.

For O'Neill's effort to cast into drama form what he is evidently so determined to say, I have unbounded admiration, though I think that in doing so he is losing precious time.

Dynamo (and this is the second way of looking at it) adds nothing to our knowledge of the religious problem. If it fails to do this, and if at the same time it fails, as it almost entirely does, to move us as a spectacle to be enjoyed in a theater, then O'Neill is clearly on the wrong track.

Our final estimate of any play does not depend on the number of particular merits or demerits we charge to its account, and in the case of *Dynamo* it takes far more time to enumerate the faults than the virtues; so I refused to see in it, as some critics did when it was shown in the theater, a proof that O'Neill was lost to us as an artist. His power as a playwright was unimpaired.

MOURNING BECOMES ELECTRA

No NEW play produced during my years of play-going has received such enthusiastic praise as *Mourning Becomes Electra*. The New York reviewers exhausted their superlatives, and left little for anyone to add about the printed text except such qualifications as the literary critics may have cared to make or such adverse comments as they may have been moved to utter.

Mourning Become Electra is no ordinary play. It is essentially different from the other late works of O'Neill, being neither a poem, nor a slice of life, nor a dramatized philosophy, nor the evocation of a mood: externally, it is a retelling of the tragic tale of Agamemnon and Clytemnestra, Orestes and Electra; an almost contemporary rearrangement of the first two parts of the Æschylean trilogy, with a curiously modern interpretation of the theme of *The Furies* (or *The Eumenides*, depending on which translation is consulted). But it is not an exemplification of the Greek religious problem of fate, for O'Neill has reconceived the old doctrine of Nemesis in terms of the more or less modern biological and psychological doctrine of cause and effect: here no mortal has offended a divinity; it is an American New Englander, a puritan, who has transgressed the moral code of his time and people, and the son of his victim turns upon the living representatives of his family for revenge. Like Abbie in *Desire Under the Elms*, Captain Brant (the counterpart of Ægistheus) becomes the helpless instrument of his own passion, and instead of seeing through to the end his bitter mission, he succumbs to the superior strength of his mistress's daughter, Lavinia (Electra), who then drives her mother to suicide, her brother Orin (Orestes) first going mad, and then killing himself. For a moment it seems as though Lavinia might find peace, but here again the heritage of hate is too heavy for her, since Orin in dying has made it impossible for his sister to marry the man she once loved. With that moral courage and single-mindedness that have sustained her throughout, she sees that death is too easy a solution for her, and with a gesture of perfect beauty and tragic serenity she turns her back on the world and walks into the house, never to come out again.

With the strange, often subtle and always interesting relationships between Lavinia and Orin in the last scenes of the third play (the whole is described as a trilogy); with the details of the family history of the Mannons and with the many overtones that are heard through the last half of the tragedy, I need not concern myself; these are matters for discussion in an extended essay, which would inquire into the artistic legitimacy of the playwright's elaboration on the General's murder, better handled in the *Agamemnon*, and of his insistence upon other scenes that would have gained in effectiveness if they had been hinted at instead of acted out. This brief survey is only an outline of the general impression created by a grandiose work, surely the most ambitious ever attempted by an American playwright. O'Neill's trilogy is a tearless tragedy, remote, detached, august, artfully shaped, cunningly devised, skillfully related and magnificently conceived. It is concerned only indirectly with life as most of us see and feel it: it is comparable not so much to music or painting as to architecture. Yet in spite of its Greek prototype its mood is Gothic rather than Greek. Its simplicity lies in its broadest outlines, which can be apprehended as we apprehend a Medieval church, only when we forget its bewildering details.

Its significance lies not in any one articulated thesis or idea, not even in the presentation of human beings in their relationships with other human beings or with society as a whole, but in the arrangement or patterning of a series of events, explained, clarified, and dramatized by an artist whose feelings and intelligence are almost completely under his control.

The play was produced by the Theatre Guild at the Guild Theatre in New York on October 26, 1931. O'Neill published in the New York *Herald Tribune* of November 3 his *Working Notes and Extracts from a Fragmentary Work Diary.*[1] These notes are of interest to anyone who cares to understand

[1] These appeared also in the "Special Edition" of the play published by Liveright in 1931, and were reprinted in my *European Theories of the Drama*, revised and expanded edition, N. Y., 1947.

the complicated problems the playwright faced and solved in the writing of his trilogy.

Were they prepared as a working guide for the playwright, or are they a brief summary of tasks faced and solved? I do not know whether O'Neill himself could now trace the precise order of development of some of the ideas that occurred to him, too slight to require a written record, but which may have been as important to him in solving his problems as those that were preserved in the notebook. But the written record is valuable as a reflection of the playwright's mental processes; it interests me not so much as showing how *Mourning Becomes Electra* was made as in reflecting an active and alert intelligence bent on expressing clearly and emphatically in the theater one of the oldest problems that man has tried to solve.

The play is no stunt. O'Neill does not trifle with the theater; even in his most obviously experimental plays the form he uses is always the result of a conscious effort to dramatize clearly some aspect of human activity. His worst mistakes are the result not of trying to see what he could do with his gifts but of his efforts to rephrase or reinterpret something he thought it worth his while to express. *Mourning Becomes Electra* is the logical outgrowth of O'Neill's other work, and closely related to it. To judge it properly, it should be looked at as part of his entire output. If you think of it this way you will see in it much more of O'Neill than of Æschylus; in spite of his deliberate use of the trilogy form and the basic similarity of the two stories, *Electra* remains a contemporary work. It presents, quite aside from its external form, another aspect of O'Neill's development not only as a writer but as a man of our day and civilization searching for a rational explanation of life and death, and what used to be called sin and evil. Directly in *Lazarus Laughed* and indirectly in *The Great God Brown, Strange Interlude, Dynamo* and *Days Without End,* O'Neill has done a lot of thinking in public, and I mean this in no derogatory sense, convinced though I am that his best plays are those that have to do not so much with expounding a philosophy as with presenting dramatically the less reflective sorts of men and women. I am here tracing his ideas rather than his development as an artist. In giving us such characters as Reuben and Dion and Nina, he is dramatizing not so much the people of our day as the abstract questions that make life an unhappy matter for so many of us. Such persons would have little reason for living if we were to accept them as human beings and not as abstractions; like their creator, they are in search of some kind of philosophy to which they can cling. Whether or not it is a formal religion that would give them power to assert themselves as positive forces in the modern world, is no matter; they think so, and thinking, rendered more complicated than ever before by the contributions of professional thinkers, is one of the most effective instruments of fate in the hands of our modern tragic writers. The characters in O'Neill's later plays are for the most part the victims, in varying degrees, of their own philosophical doubts. In *Lazarus Laughed*, however, we have a positive and joyous assertion of the will to live, a proclamation made by an idealistic prophet who is tortured by no doubts, a man so sure of his message that he has actually banished death from his world. But O'Neill took good care to put this prophet into a world far remote from us, a world nearly two thousand years younger than it is now. *Lazarus Laughed* is not life; it is the playwright's dream between an earlier and a later hell on earth. That the philosophy of this play is not sufficient to its author is shown by the writer's later efforts to find and express a more substantial faith.

There would be no point in comparing the O'Neill play with the Æschylus trilogy if it were not that the attempt sheds light on the American's attitude toward his aims as a writer. O'Neill turned to Æschylus because the Greek had ready to hand a set of conventions that enabled him to present certain aspects of life that seemed important, without having to explain too much of the background or history of his characters. The chorus, the masks, the formal literary language,

the common heritage of history, legend, religion, politics—
such were among the advantages enjoyed by the ancient Greek
dramatists, who were not much concerned with the surfaces
of things and the accidentals of daily existence. Greek tragedy
offered O'Neill a wider field for the expression of his ideas
'than he could have had if he had chosen a modern scene and
modern characters. Mere realism, observation, reporting, were
not what he was after. "Too many playwrights," he said to
me when we were talking this over shortly after he had finished writing *Electra*, "are intent upon writing about people,
instead of life." Even in his earlier plays you can see O'Neill
reaching out beyond the framework he had set himself before
he was able to aim higher, and it is for this reason that even in
such well-rounded plays as *Desire Under the Elms* I never feel
quite satisfied that the playwright was himself satisfied. What
appeals to me most strongly in those of his plays I most respect
and like is this uneasy undertone that hints at something not
completely expressed. The dramatic poet need not always expound his theory of life.

In turning to Greek tragedy for a medium through which
he might express dramatically another aspect of one of the
problems of modern life, O'Neill was determined to reduce
his story to its barest outlines and his characters to their quin-
tessential selves, either divining or having read in Aristotle
that in tragedy "character comes in as subsidiary to the actions," since the "incidents and the plot are the end of tragedy; and the end is the chief thing of all." Precisely as in *The
Great God Brown* he had avoided showing us the individual
peculiarities of facial expression through the use of masks,
and in *Strange Interlude* and *Dynamo* resorted to the aside
and the soliloquy because he wanted to get at the mental
processes of his people without making every speech seem "natural," so in *Mourning Becomes Electra* he used a ready-made
story into all the details and motives and reasons of which it
was not necessary to go. If he had lived in Elizabethan England, he would probably have gone over to the Bankside and

written plays in blank verse. He admits that what his new play needs is immortal poetry, and he is modest enough to confess that he was not the man to write it.

When, therefore, he wrote in his *Notes and Extracts from a Fragmentary Diary* that it had occurred to him to write a "modern psychological drama using one of the old legend plots of Greek tragedy," it was no sudden inspiration, but the culmination of a series of technical experiments, patient quests in search of a method. Follow these notes, begun in 1926, and you will see that O'Neill soon made up his mind to use Æschylus only when Æschylus could help, and to fall back on O'Neill for the rest.

His earliest problem was outlined in the first note: "Is it possible to get modern psychological approximation of Greek sense of fate into such a play, which an intelligent audience of today, possessed by no belief in gods or moral retribution, could accept and be moved by?"

This must have given him no little trouble. After all, Æschylus did write for an audience that accepted a set of more or less established moral, religious, and political dogmas, and it was not necessary for him to answer such questions as an modern American audience must have answered before they will accept the premises laid down in a play. And we must remember that the *Oresteia* was based upon legends as familiar to fifth-century Athens as the Bible stories were to Puritan New England. Your fundamentalist never thinks of asking about Adam's parentage; he knows.

O'Neill soon saw that he could not very well place his story against a present-day background; the time of the Civil War was just remote enough. "Civil War," he noted, "is only possibility—fits into picture—Civil War as background for drama of murderous family love and hate." Yet that epoch is far enough removed for us to accept certain conventions without demanding a meticulous explanation for every motive, but close enough to enable us to identify ourselves with the ideas and emotions of the characters. Æschylus could take it for granted that his audience knew what the Trojan War was about, so O'Neill had only to suggest *his* time and place, knowing that he need not explain much about the Civil War, or a New England city.

The *Agamemnon* and *Homecoming* (the first part of the O'Neill trilogy) are concerned with situations that are fundamentally alike. In Æschylus' play, Agamemnon returns to his wife Clytemnestra, who has been unfaithful to him with Ægistheus, Agamemnon's cousin; Clytemnestra murders him because he has sacrificed their daughter Iphigenia, because he brings home with him a concubine, and because she wants Ægistheus to rule over the kingdom. In the O'Neill play, Ezra Mannon returns to his wife Christine, who has been unfaithful to him with Captain Adam Brant, Ezra's cousin; Christine murders him because she has always hated him and wants to marry Adam.

Neither Electra nor Orestes has a place in the Greek play, and Orestes is scarcely mentioned; he is no more than an ominous note in a speech of Cassandra's, and in one of the choral chants. In omitting Cassandra and the choruses (except for the modern counterpart of the townspeople, who are used chiefly as background), and in not suggesting a direct parallel to the sacrifice of Iphigenia, O'Neill had to furnish some substitute for the material introduced into the ancient story by these means, not because he was trying to "modernize" Æschylus, but because he was establishing a dramatic embodiment of the fate that pursued the house of Mannon. The fact that Clytemnestra was jealous of Cassandra is of little importance, and the sacrifice of Iphigenia—for O'Neill's purpose—is just as irrelevant. So, instead of making Orestes the chief instrument of vengeance, as Æschylus did in the second part of his trilogy, he at once gave to Lavinia the combined dramatic functions of the prophetess, the avenger Orestes, and the choruses. It is she who learns the story of the feud between Ezra's grandfather Abe and his brother David; who learns that her mother's lover Brant is the son of David and the servant girl Marie Brantome; and because she is an inevitable product of the combined hatreds of her parents and their parents in turn, she cannot rest until she has pursued the guilty parties to their final punishment. She will see to it that they pay the price of sin.

The Greek legend tells that Atreus and Thyestes, sons of Pelops, "dwelt at Argos with Eurystheus the king . . . and when he died, Atreus ruled in his place, and wedded his daughter. But Thyestes wronged his brother's wife, and was banished from Argos. And after a while he returned again, and clung unto the altar at Argos; and Atreus, fearing to slay him, devised this deed. He slew certain of the children of Thyestes, and bade him to a banquet, and gave him to eat of his own children's flesh; and he ate, knowing not what it was. But when he knew what was done, he spake a bitter curse upon the house of Atreus, that they should all perish by a doom like that of his own children. And there befell these woes unto that house, and for three generations the curse of murder departed not away."

Not for a moment does the Greek poet allow us to forget that because of the first sin of Thyestes and Atreus the gods have decreed and sought retribution and suffering from the guilty. With occasionally tiresome insistence, chorus after chorus repeats the dirge of that

> impious deed
> From which that after-growth of ill doth rise.

Whereas with Æschylus the first play ends with the temporary triumph of Clytemnestra, with O'Neill Christine stands already charged with murder by her daughter, a woman whom we feel at once to be mistress of the situation.

The Libation-Bearers, the second play of the Greek trilogy, introduces Orestes and Electra, but the woman soon fades into the background and Orestes undertakes alone to pursue his mother and her lover. He has consulted the Delphic oracle and is commanded by Apollo to punish the guilty pair, in accordance with the decree of Zeus; he acts quickly, with the help of his friend Pylades, but almost immediately after the double murder he is beset by the avenging Furies, symbols of yet another power not under the control of Zeus and at variance with the laws of the Olympian hierarchy, and he is driven mad.

In O'Neill's second play, *The Hunted*, we follow up to a certain point the same broad course of events: Lavinia and her brother Orin together track down Christine and Adam, kill the man, and drive their mother to suicide. In the belief that her mission is ended Lavinia turns to her temporarily unbalanced brother, determined at last to find happiness, and ultimately to marry the normal and unimaginative Peter. But she has reckoned without the Furies, those powerful and as yet not fully understood forces within us that wreck mind and body when they are no longer under control. Orin, being the weaker, is the first to succumb. His case is complicated by a certain introspective malady that was unknown to or at least not touched upon by Æschylus.

At this point O'Neill declares his virtual independence of the Greek model. Æschylus carried him as far as was necessary. It would have been useless and absurd to attempt to utilize to any great extent a modern counterpart to *The Furies*, the third part of the Greek trilogy. I confess I find this play anticlimactic. It is in some respects a political and patriotic document, and in writing the last part of it, the Greek poet side-stepped the moral and psychological problems he had raised and up to that point developed. What, we wonder and demand to know, will Orestes do, torn between two opposed forces, the one a command from the chief of the gods, the other a personified urge from the irresistible goddesses of vengeance? It was fated that such-and-such events should come to pass, that the family of Atreus should suffer for the wrongs committed by certain of its members; yet to make doubly sure that he was the instrument ordained to punish the guilty, Orestes had scrupulously performed his re-

...us duties and consulted the oracle, presumably the highest source of religious authority. His God commanded him to do the deed, yet upon committing it he found he had transgressed another law, decreed by the Furies. For a man in such a dilemma the only way out, according to Æschylus, was to appeal to the highest court in the most enlightened country: Æschylus' country, and the local court of the Areopagus at Athens.

Instead of facing the issue, or carrying it to some higher source of moral justice, or even leaving it unsolved among those problems that men simply cannot fathom, he shows us Orestes appealing to Athena, the patron goddess of the very city whose people made up Æschylus' audience:

> I call Athena, lady of this land
> To come, my champion.

Verily, Athena was no less obliging to the Greeks than the United States marines used to be to our melodramatists, never allowing a gallant hero to remain long in the hands of wicked foreigners. But the Furies are no less insistent upon their rights, Athena or no Athena; for it is their claim that matricide is punishable by annihilation, no matter what the motive that prompted it. A jury of Athenian citizens is summoned by the goddess, court is held on the Areopagus (in sight of the theater where the *Oresteia* was performed) and Orestes is tried. Portia-like, and very much at home in her own city, the goddess addresses the Furies: "The form of justice, not its deed, thou willest." The jury is divided, but Athena, who herself decreed that she should have the deciding vote in case of a tie, absolves her suppliant. The Furies complain:

> Now are they all undone, the ancient laws
> ... New wrong for ancient right shall be
> If matricide go free.

A long argument follows, and at last the Furies consent not only to accept the verdict, but to be friendly, for Athena promises them "great honor from the Athenians, and a sacred dwelling in the land . . . , and they were appeased, and were called·no more Furies, but Gracious Goddesses." Orestes virtually disappears from the play at this point, as Æschylus brings his trilogy to its wordy closing scene. The opposing parties are reconciled by acknowledging the supremacy of the Athenian tribunal in matters of religion and state. That this was propaganda to strengthen the prestige of the Athenian court at a moment when it was threatened by the popular party is well known. The Father of Drama has avoided the very issues he raised, either because he could not make up his mind as to whether Orestes was guilty or not, or because he cared more about the government of his own city than he did about his trilogy.

In the third O'Neill play, *The Haunted*, the playwright parts company almost entirely from Æschylus. He might, of course, by way of furnishing a counterpart to *The Furies*, have taken Lavinia and Orin before the Supreme Court at Washington, and introduced an archbishop instructing the nine justices as to what procedure they should adopt in dealing with the culprits; only he would have had to reduce the number of justices to eight or increase it to ten and made the Statue of Liberty the final arbiter in case of a tie. Further, the jury would have to be told it would remain forever, under proper religious guidance, the ultimate standard of all human conduct:

> . . . Man with man and state with state
> Shall vow the pledge of common hate
> And common friendship, that for man
> Hath oft made blessing out of ban,
> Be ours unto all time.

The decrees of Fate, or its modern equivalent, may nowadays be stated quite as easily as that, but they are not accepted as they may have been twenty-three hundred years ago.

, whatever may be thought of O'Neill's purely literary achievement as compared with the poetry of Æschylus, I for one am ready to give the American the wreath of laurel or the cask of wine that goes to the victor, for working out his fate motif with greater skill and more courage and a deeper understanding of the human mind than the Greek had done. O'Neill was at least after the truth as he saw it, while Æschylus sought the less honorable course of glorifying his state and its official religion.

Instead of avenging Furies, placated by a mere bribe (this at least is a modern touch), O'Neill gives us an exhibition of complexes, a picture of moral and mental struggle that, in its broad aspects, is acceptable to us of today. The playwright saw the thing through, whether we happen to like his solution or not.

From the *Notes* it appears that O'Neill found it hard at first to set forth in dramatic form some modern equivalent for the Furies, but he got the cue from his own observation and experience, intensified and clarified by a certain amount of scientific reading. In the first draft, not so abstract or formal as the final one, he had come close to the methods of naturalism, but as he dug deeper into his subject, he found the play "sprouting out," as he wrote me at the time, "into a technique more uniquely belonging to me and my theme, and I am highly excited with the possibilties. However, I don't want you to think I am . . . reaching out after something strange and new. It is really only a development and combination of methods I have successfully used before."

While Æschylus conducted his matricide into the arms of a politically prejudiced goddess who tried him by unfair means and absolved him from guilt in order to glorify Athens, O'Neill focused his attention on Lavinia, plus Orin (these two being his Orestes). Lavinia, the product of those very forces in her family which precipitated its peculiar and inevitable fate, discovers that she has at last become like her own mother, that in demanding payment for sin that grew out of lust and hatred she herself is inevitably drawn to her own brother and even to the naked savages, now that her father, toward whom she was also drawn by forces not exactly filial, is no longer alive. All her natural instincts, thwarted by a maniacal desire for vengeance, have turned in upon her. This is her fate, and she marches to a doom which is actually inescapable, from which no god-from-the-machine, no benign court, no accommodating dramatist, is able to save her. For such victims of the evil that seems inherent in life there is no salvation.

Instead of using masks to show what has happened to Orin and Lavinia, O'Neill simply states in his stage directions that they have come to resemble their parents, a bit of symbolism more strikingly dramatic than he could have achieved if he had actually made the actors put on masks. "I'm now," says Orin, "in Father's place and you're Mother. . . . That's the evil destiny out of the past I haven't dared predict! I'm the Mannon you're chained to!" Out of the mouth of this demented man has come the ultimate truth. Like the inspired Cassandra, he perceives through his disordered mind the meaning of the curse.

So the last of the Mannons, like Abbie and Eben in *Desire Under the Elms,* have become the instruments of their own fate.

For a time it seemed that each would find happiness in love, Lavinia with Peter, and Orin with Hazel; happiness, too, loomed for them in the distant isles, those hazy dream refuges that recur from time to time in the tortured visions of the brother and his sister, but because each was a Mannon, damned by the Mannon tradition and temperament and a knowledge of the Mannon history, each had to pay the price. *The Haunted* is largely concerned with the exposition of the introspective tragedies of a man and a woman observed and studied to a certain extent in the light of modern science. That the revelations of this science were expressed and patterned somewhat too precisely after Freud and Jung I felt on first reading the play, but O'Neill's answer to my criticism is worth quoting:

> I don't agree with your Freudian objection. Taken from my author's angle, I find fault with critics on exactly the same point—that they read too damn much Freud into stuff that could very well have been written exactly as is before psychoanalysis was ever heard of. Imagine the Freudian bias that would be read into Stendhal, Balzac, Strindberg, Dostoievsky, etc., if they were writing today! After all, every human complication of love and hate in my trilogy is as old as literature, and the interpretations I suggest are such as might have occurred to any author in any time with a deep curiosity about the underlying motives that actuate human interrelationships in the family. In short, I think I know enough about men and women to have written *Mourning Becomes Electra* almost exactly as it is if I had never heard of Freud or Jung or the others. Authors were psychologists, you know, and profound ones, before psychology was invented. And I am no deep student of psychoanalysis. As far as I can remember, of all the books written by Freud, Jung, etc., I have read only four, and Jung is the only one of the lot who interests me. Some of his suggestions I find extraordinarily illuminating in the light of my own experience with hidden human motives.

The whole question of this treatment of the theme of fate in modern life as compared with its treatment by the ancient Greek dramatic poets is worth discussing only for the light it sheds on the fundamental problem O'Neill asked himself in the note already quoted: "Is it possible to get modern psychological approximation of Greek sense of fate into such a play" which would be accepted by modern audiences? Modern audiences, says O'Neill, have no general religious basis, no common fund of tradition to which they may refer the greatest problems with which we are all concerned. The closest modern equivalent is our yet-infant science of psychology; fate, says O'Neill, is what happens to human beings because of what they are, not what some god tells them to be, and it is the business of the tragic dramatist to show how human destiny reacts upon the individual, the family, the race.

That science may be wrong, that the little we know about ourselves is ridiculously far from the ultimate truth, is no matter; every generation must restate and try to reinterpret the human story and the human tragedy as best it may.

AH, WILDERNESS!

"THE PLAYWRIGHT," Burns Mantle tells us (*The Best Plays of 1933–34*), "had been working unusually hard on his *Days Without End*. When he had finished the third draft he determined to put that drama aside and rest for a week. He awoke next morning with the story, characters, plot scheme and practically all the details of *Ah, Wilderness!* in his mind clamoring to be put down on paper. O'Neill went back to work and within a month had completed a first draft of *Ah, Wilderness!* Then he went on with *Days Without End*. When this much more difficult drama was finally ready to be delivered to the Guild O'Neill took out the first draft of *Ah, Wilderness!* and was startled to find that, so far as he could judge, the first draft was quite as good as he could make it. He brought the play with him to New York and submitted it to the Guild directorate. They not only bought it on sight, but put in into rehearsal within a week."

The play opened in October, 1933, became a popular success and ran through the season. It was written in Georgia in 1932. Characterized by its author as "a dream walking," and "a comedy of recollection" it is a nostalgic family comedy, laid in a small Connecticut city in 1906. There are no philosophical implications in this simple serious comedy, and there is scarcely a hint of ironic intention; it comes rather as a quiet interlude in the work of a playwright who had not so far in his writing career been content to use the theater merely as a means of showing character detached, as it were, from the ulterior complications of human existence. He was not again, up to the present moment, to make another attempt of the same kind. "My purpose," he writes in a short note in *The Wilderness Edition,* "was to write a play true to the spirit of the American large small-town at the turn of the century. Its quality depended upon atmosphere, sentiment, an exact evocation of the mood of a dead past. To me, the America which was (and is) the real America found its unique expression in such middle-class families as the Millers, among whom so many of my own generation passed from adolescence into manhood."

Young Richard Miller, an introspective youth "going on seventeen, just out of high school," is something of a family problem. "Poetry's his red meat nowadays . . . love poetry— and socialism, too, I suspect, from some dire declarations he's made." And sex as well, and the state of the world in general. He's fond of the equally immature Muriel McComber, whose father reacts in true bourgeois fashion when he discovers that the youth has been sending her love poems by Swinburne, and other "vile" and inflammatory missives. When the girl writes him a letter putting an end to their friendship, the lad becomes a full-blown pessimist. By way of proving to himself the genuineness of his disillusion he walks out of the house and in a low dive meets a prostitute, buys drinks for her and for himself, and discovers that he can go no further with her down the road to ruin: timidity and disgust, a certain self-respect and a chivalrous consideration for Muriel, all keep him "pure." But he does make his appearance before his assembled family in a shocking state of drunkenness. When, a little later, he sees Muriel again and learns that her letter had been dictated by Papa and that she is still fond of him, he tells her frankly of his misdeeds, and the two are reconciled.

The comedy is not primarily a study in anything; the plot, as outlined, is only a part of what the playwright was interested in. It is a fairly broad canvas, upon which a pretty detailed domestic scene is painted. O'Neill has here accurately and affectionately summoned from the depths of his memory the mothers and fathers, the aunts, brothers, friends and neighbors and servants whose everyday concerns and small-talk, whose little comedies and tragedies, made up the sum-total of the kind of middle-class family to which he and his contemporaries belonged some fifty years ago.

The fact that O'Neill thought it worth his while to write *Ah, Wilderness!* at all, without straining to give it a partic-ular direction and inner meaning, is, I think, of some impor-tance in any consideration of his entire output.

DAYS WITHOUT END

Ah, Wilderness!, as I have pointed out, was written after O'Neill had put aside the third draft of *Days Without End.* He intended to take a week's rest. Instead, he wrote a first draft of the new comedy; then he went back again to *Days Without End.* Even a quick reading of this play will show why its author needed rest: it is probably the most baldly intellectual, closely reasoned work he ever wrote; the most explicitly reasoned and logically presented. And at the same time, and perhaps for those very reasons, by all odds the dullest as a stage play.

Written in Georgia in 1932 and 1933, it was produced by the Theatre Guild early in January, 1934, and ran at the Henry Miller Theater for only fifty-seven performances. By and large, it was a great disappointment, except to a few persons who were pleased to see in it not only a plea for Catholicism but clear evidence that its author had returned to the faith of his childhood. If O'Neill had in fact decided to resolve all the philosophic doubts that had bedevilled him —and through him, so many of the protagonists of his plays; had, indeed, re-embraced a faith which would effectively cure the "sickness of today," as he puts it, he would probably not have gone to the trouble of writing so elaborate a treatise as

Days Without End. In his *Eugene O'Neill, a Critical Study,* (1934) Sophus Keith Winther writes: "If it is a failure as an acting play [and this, he argues, is only relatively true] or if its concluding scene is unconvincing, the critical implications of the whole argument reveal a mind alive to the limitations and the values of the past, a mind high-strung and intense, keyed to new ventures and further explorations." In other words, O'Neill is still seeking an answer to man's quest for spiritual certainty. A brief recital of the "plot" of this play can give no proper notion of such intrinsic value as it may have as an index to the author's mental processes and spiritual struggles, but it does suggest some of its esthetic shortcomings as a dramatic production.

The play is about John Loving; two personalities are present within him, and in everlasting conflict one with the other. One of them is known simply as John, the other as Loving, and each is played by a different actor. John is the external man, the only one seen by the audience and the other persons in the play; Loving is seen only by the audience and John. It is Loving who represents or voices the scepticism that tortures John, who embodies the religious doubts which prevent John from achieving the solace of an unquestioned faith. When John's parents died, years before, the young man's belief in a benevolent God had died in him. Never satisfied for long by any answer he could wring from philosophy or religion, and refusing to accept the consolation which his priest uncle has for years been trying to bring to him, he has married and in his wife Elsa he found temporary solace; to him "God is love." Yet, driven by complicated motives, by an introspective and sadistic desire to explore further the basic meaning of things—specifically, by what may be called his "baser" nature—he is false to his new God; he is unfaithful to the wife whom he loves. He has written a novel about himself, his past struggles and his attempts to find an answer to his uncertainties, and in telling the plot of it to Elsa and his uncle, he confesses what he has done; and Elsa, when she learns of her husband's infidelity, falls ill, and is about to die. She cannot forgive John, and she will make no effort to live. John, still at war with Loving, and struggling against his own scepticism and also against the priest's attempts to bring him back to the faith of his boyhood, cannot face the fact of his wife's death, particularly since he holds himself responsible for her condition. Apparently there is no other way to save her life—indeed his own life as well. Yet Elsa finds it in her heart to forgive him, and from that moment on we learn that the crisis is over, and she will survive. The last scene, a short one, is the interior of a church, the stage dominated by a large crucifix. John comes in, accompanied by the still rebellious but considerably weakened Loving; he falls to his knees at the foot of the cross, and begs forgiveness. "I have come back to Thee," he sobs. "Let me believe in Thy love again!" Then "His eyes fixed on the face of the Crucified suddenly lighting up as if he now saw there the answer to his prayer . . .", he feels he is forgiven, that he can at last forgive himself; he can indeed believe. Loving "slumps to his knees beside John, as if some invisible force crushed him down." The sceptic has been conquered. "Thou art—the End. Forgive—the damned soul—of John Loving!" He falls dead, "his head beneath the foot of the Cross, his arms outflung so that his body forms another Cross." No longer is the soul of John Loving divided; "John" is not John plus Loving, but John Loving, a man at last whole, at peace with himself. "Love lives forever!" he cries, and the play closes as John tells the priest that "Life laughs with God's love again. Life laughs with love!"

Days Without End, however useful it may be as a guide to O'Neill's development as playwright and man, is a very poor play; it is slow-moving, almost wholly unconvincing in the theater, never for a moment animated by the breath of life. As in a Medieval morality play, the characters are pure abstractions who utter speeches which must be analyzed in the light of what has gone before and remembered clearly in the light of what is to follow. In spite of two or three short scenes that are somewhat moving, we are left cold and unmoved by the play as an entity. The concluding scene in the church is wholly contrived and melodramatic.

It is possible that *Days Without End* might have been made into a play, but as it stands I can see in it only a diagrammatic outline for an unwritten work. In discussing it with Mr. Nathan some years after it was produced, O'Neill said that the "hero's final gesture calls for alteration." Whether he referred to the dramatic gesture in the last scene, or his mental "gesture" in returning to the Catholic faith, I cannot say.

TEMPORARY RETIREMENT, 1934–1946

I DO NOT intend to follow in detail the playwright's travels, nor his plans, nor his many bouts of illness, nor his writing labors between the year 1934, when *Days Without End* was first seen in the theater, and 1946, when *The Iceman Cometh* opened in New York. It was a period of almost incredible activity. There is no point in recording here the details of the twelve years' existence of Mr. and Mrs. O'Neill, some of them spent in Georgia, some on the West Coast, all of them spent in quiet seclusion. Nor is there any use in trying to establish in chronological order the conception or writing of each play or group of plays. I shall rely mostly on excerpts from letters sent to me by O'Neill from time to time, though from these I am excluding much that throws light on his personal life and several that explain his development as an artist. Some of the letters which I am not using would properly fit into a more detailed study than I have attempted in this book, but a great many I have left out for purely practical reasons. To begin with, the letters written to me are of course by no means a complete record of work done; they were not intended for publication; and if they are ever to be so used, they must be checked against other letters. I don't ask

O'Neill, when he takes it into his head to tell me what he is doing or thinking, whether or not he is talking for publication. Such considerations cramp anyone's style.

The O'Neills, as I have already said, moved to Georgia in 1932, building a house at Sea Island Beach which they called Casa Genotta. In the latter part of 1936 they left and went to Seattle. In the following year they moved to Contra Costa County, near Berkeley, California, where they built another place, which they called Tao House. There they lived until 1944, when they moved to a small hotel in San Francisco. Early in 1946 they came to New York, lived in a Mid-town hotel for some weeks, and then took a lease on an apartment where, O'Neill tells me, they are "settled"—for how long no one, I think, can say.

Public announcements in the press, an occasional interview, private letters to his friends and business representatives would fill in the picture here far more clearly and accurately than will the quotations I am selecting for these pages, but these will at least give a fair account of O'Neill's work and some notion of his attitude toward that work and toward the world in which he has been living.

Shortly before leaving Georgia he wrote, on March 3, 1936, "I'm slaving on my damned Cycle, as I have been over a year now—the greater part of that time on scenarios and preliminary work. Have one play almost completed but I'm not going to release anything for production until at least three are done."

Periods of illness and intense work followed. It was not until September of the following year that I had further direct news. The O'Neills were then settled in Contra Costa County, and the letterhead bears the postal address of Lafayette: "I begin to feel something like myself. Have begun to flirt with my Cycle of plays again—with many fresh ideas and angles, including still another play which carries the beginning back to 1775, and will make nine plays in all. There will be nothing of *Ah, Wilderness!* or *Days Without*

End in this Cycle. They were an interlude. The Cycle goes back to my old vein of ironic tragedy—with, I hope, added psychological depth and insight. The whole work will be a unique something, all right, believe me, if I can ever finish it. As you will appreciate, the technical problem alone is overpowering—of keeping each play a unit in itself while at the same time making it a vital part of the whole conception. I have to think in terms of nine plays, and a continuity of family lives over a space of 150 years, while I am writing each play. But given time and health I can do it. What I would like to do is not have any production until the whole thing is finished . . . productions are only nerve-racking interruptions to me—'show business'—and never have meant anything more. The play, as written, is the thing, and not the way actors garble it with their almost-always-alien personalities (even when the acting is fine work in itself). But whether circumstances will permit my abstention from production for such a long time remains to be seen. The present status of the Cycle is one play (the third now) in good shape, needing only revising; another play (formerly the first, now the second) in a first draft as long as *Interlude,* needing complete rewriting. All the rest well thought out and scenarioed with much detail. And eight hundred million notes—more or less! I am going easy on work yet, however, and warily, because I still must watch my step and not risk a slide backwards. But by the first of the year I hope to be ready to really drive ahead."

A little over a week later O'Neill acknowledged receipt of a little preface of mine printed with a translation of a play of Romain Rolland. I had drawn parallels between the situation in contemporary Russia and the period in France when the Robespierres and his kind were "liquidating" the earlier leaders. "A true play," he wrote, "about the French Revolution ought to make a grand satire on the Russian one. Or . . . a play or novel depicting the history of any religion would apply rationally in the same way. God with a change of whiskers becomes the State—and then there's always a Holy Book

—dogmas—heresy trials—an infallible Pope—etc.—etc., until you become sick. It appears we apes always climb trees—and fall out of them—with a boringly identical behavior pattern!" In a P.S. to the same letter he adds: "The last of the above sounds pessimistic—whereas I feel full of hope these days. For, noting the way the world wags, I am sure that Man has definitely decided to destroy himself, and this seems to me the only truly wise decision he has ever made!"

A few more letters serve to fill the gap until early March of 1941, but the next quotation is from a letter dated March 27th in that year. I had, as usual, expressed the hope that he would allow at least some of his work to be seen in the theater, and I had told him that not only "we" in New York needed him but it was possible that contact with the theater might keep him in touch with the mechanics of production—to his advantage. Of course, I didn't express my thought quite so directly; besides, I knew that once he had made up his mind, argument would not move him. So, in the March 1941 letter, he reported on work in progress, and said little, except by indirection, about coming East or having anything to do with the theater. "Regarding work," he wrote, "I've finished two plays outside the Cycle in the past two years, and I'm enthusiastic about them. Both will rank among the few very best things I've ever done, I know. I've also worked now and then on the Cycle. Principally notes of fresh angles, new outlines, etc. So while on the shelf, pending a return of sanity and future to our groggy world, it is still very much alive and reorienting itself in my mind, as it needs to do if it is to express the conceptions the changing times force on the change in me. So much has happened, without and within, since I started to write it. The stories of the separate plays aren't affected much, but the vision of life that binds them into a whole has bogged down in shifting uncertainties. As for the production of the new outside plays, I have no idea when. Not soon, I know. A matter of my health mostly. The past winter has been the worst since my crack-up in '37. One thing after another. I've been able to do little in the past four months except detailed outlines of three new plays—all non-cycle, of course. But I'm feeling better now that the much advertised California sun has returned to California, where it wasn't, except for a few days, in several months. There's a large lack of inclination about production, too. Somehow, in these times, it just doesn't strike me as mattering whether or not. All I really care about is to stay here and write. The thought of New York gives me the pip."

A few more letters came within the next couple of years, some of them on minor matters of business, others having to do with O'Neill's thoughts about radio, the use of his plays by non-professional acting groups; my plan to reprint his father's version of *Monte Cristo* in a collection of old plays. Though I am not printing any of these letters, there is one, in particular, concerned with the problem of keeping a large establishment going in wartime without servants, that shows O'Neill's amused concern with what to less intense artists would amount to passing trivialities. Not only were the O'Neills forced to prepare their own meals (he writes that in wiping dishes he hasn't "broken a single one yet, so help me!"), they discovered in their new way of life that they were living in a community, and that the playwright was perhaps not able, as he had hoped, to command a privacy so complete as he had dreamed of when he took to his hill-top. And I feel that the contact he established with local people ("not the rich estate people of the countryside"), somehow helped restore the man's essential faith in a world which his reading and contemplation had, in a way, distorted. As a matter of fact, I began, at the time when this letter came to me in early September of 1943, to feel that O'Neill's mind was far more pessimistic than his dramas; his thinking was occasionally defeatist when his deepest feelings were probably not. He goes on in this letter to say that he and Mrs. O'Neill would not have been able to remain at Tao House but for the friendly help of the "small-town business men, small farmers, etc.—the forgotten 'class' . . . we have always liked these people . . . and evidently they have liked us, for they have shown a kindness money cannot buy and gone out of their way to help us."

About his writing activities he reports again: "Although I have done no writing lately, my record since Pearl Harbor is not as poor as it might be. I have finished, except for a final cutting, another non-Cycle play—*A Moon for the Misbegotten*—and rewritten the 1928 Cycle play—*A Touch of the Poet*, done some work off and on on another non-Cycle— *The Last Conquest*—anti-totalitarian state, anti-Instrumentalist philosophy, but useless as present war propaganda because it is a symbolic fantasy of the future, and of the last campaign for the final destruction of the spirit—which (happy ending) does not succeed. When, in addition, I consider *The Iceman Cometh*, most of which was written after war started in '39, and *Long Day's Journey Into Night*, written the following year—(these two plays give me greater satisfaction than any other two I've ever done)—and a one-act play, *Hughie*, one of a series of eight I want to do under the general title, *By Way of Obit*, I feel I've done pretty well in the four war years. I go into the above details to assure you that, until lately, I have not been upset by war, sickness, or anything else to the point where I have quit on my job." A short P.S. to the same letter reads: "Started this letter weeks ago. Have been laid up in bed—still all in but up for awhile to-day. *But* we have just got a cook, so that cancels the bad breaks—that is, if she stays!"

Again, this time from a family hotel in San Francisco, February 22, 1944, in answer to something I had written about *Lazarus Laughed*. I don't remember what I had said, but it was something about a production of that play in revised form. "I am . . . pleased," he wrote, "by your reference to *Lazarus Laughed*—except I think what you feel is not only implicit but also explicit in it; that in spite of its obscuring overload of masked pageantry it manages to state a spiritual warning and hope which could be important to-day. Recently—and not for the first time—I have tried to get the Guild interested in a Lazarus production—that is, in a cut, condensed version with masks omitted. Choruses, a choir, small parts almost entirely cut out, crowds done by off-stage choral effect, etc. Simplest way to explain my idea is, you remember the opera, *Boris Gudinoff*? Well, along that line, but not opera as far as main characters are concerned, except that Lazarus' laughter becomes transformed into music. (I believe in the Pasadena production they tried to do a little of what I mean.) However, it is foolish to think of it. Not a chance. And, after all, I can't blame the producers. Who could do inspiring choral music for such a production? I don't know. Who could direct it? I can't answer that one either. Above all, who could play Lazarus? Since Chaliapin died, I can't think of anyone. He could have done it—and how!—for he was a magnificent actor, a tremendous personality on the stage. He sang, but he could also give speech the quality of music—and that's exactly what Lazarus must do. Trouble with *Lazarus Laughed* is what you said years ago in your criticism. Too much pageantry, too much repetition in talk, too long for itself. But these are faults easily corrected. Also, I don't like the title."

The next letter, also from San Francisco, is dated December 15, 1944. It was in answer to an inquiry I had received from one of the universities, asking for permission to produce *Strange Interlude*. O'Neill was willing to allow the director to go ahead. "I haven't read the play," he said, "since it was produced, save for excerpts here and there, but I don't think much of it will 'date' that is really important, and certainly Nina's reactions to her aviator lover's death should be closer to to-day's audience than the '28 one of forgetfulness and the Big Boom . . . unless my memory is wrong, the play as printed in my book is longer than the Theatre Guild acting script. I made cuts for time, also because some dialogue was condensed for the stage, but I thought it should be retained in the original for a reader of the book. I've done this with quite a few of my plays. On the other hand, I made too many cuts in *Mourning Becomes Electra* and let too many of them (but not all) stay in the book. It was a fuller, better play in its final written version, I think. And so with *Ah, Wilderness!* It was a better portrayal of a family in its final written version. I never thought then of having a star in it. Even in its present book version with the cuts, it has always been given in Europe with the boy as the main figure—and successfully." In the same letter O'Neill goes on again about *Lazarus Laughed:* "The story of my cut version of 'Lazarus Laughed' is fable. It's true I've thought of different ways it might be cut and simplified—for example, cut my complicated mask scheme—no double-sized mask idea for Chorus—all crowds done by off stage effects—cuts in the repetitious chants and all these given to the Chorus—many of the minor characters cut out—concentration on Lazarus, Tiberius, Caligula, etc. with chorus background—music to sustain Lazarus' laughter and that of others, as if this music sprang from their laughter, went along with it, dominated it, and finally became pure music with no voice or voices left. Well, you get the idea. Take all the pageantry of my immense 'Imaginative Theatre' stadium out. Make it simple, all to be put on in a modern large theatre, the symbolic story of Lazarus' brief second life on earth, and the message he brought back from the tomb. There's no chance of my doing this now. I'm too ill. I haven't done any work in a long time, although there is a lot writing to be done. I can't take any interest in it."

Incidentally, the university never got round to doing *Strange Interlude*, nor *Lazarus Laughed*, though the author's suggestions on both plays were passed on to the theater director. In another part of the letter just quoted from, O'Neill says that if the nonprofessional group wants to try working with *Lazarus*, it will have his blessing. "I think it is just the kind of job they ought to try. It's hard and it's technically creative. They would have my general conception of what

ought to be done, but it is up to them to do it. Also, they
would be working on something practically virgin, something
Broadway never touched, the kind of thing their theatre
should stand for, an American play of the spirit, and a play
which should have a message now when death and the meaning or meaninglessness of life are so close to us. There is also
a lot of the murder, madness and death realism of Tiberius
and Caligula in Hitlerism—very much so!"

In March, 1946, I spent part of an afternoon with O'Neill
at his New York hotel. Seeing him for the first time in more
than ten years I was shocked at his appearance. He was pain-
fully thin and shrunken, and the trembling of his hands was
so marked that he had great trouble in lighting a cigarette.
He told me he could no longer write with a pen nor use a
typewriter, and was at the moment trying to learn how to use
some kind of dictograph. The words came slowly, haltingly.
This was clearly not the result of nervousness alone.[1] True,
he had told me in his letters of long and strenuous attacks of
illness, but I was not prepared to see a man who looked as
though he should be in a hospital. Then he got into his stride,
and as the talk went on I began to forget my first impression
of his appearance, and while the hands still trembled, the
sentences took shape, and the O'Neill I remembered was again
sitting before me. He spoke to the point, with complete
clarity, with good humor and graciousness, and with an almost
complete lack of self-consciousness. His interest in the world
about him seemed deeper and broader than before, he was a
little less concerned with his own plays than I had expected
he would be, even though he knew it was my business to hear
him talk about them; I detected in his conversation a sort of
tolerantly humorous attitude toward life that was somewhat
at variance with his ideas as they were worked into his plays;

[1] Parkinson's Disease has been mentioned, and it is likely that the diagnosis is
correct. It is a disease "which," among other things, "affects the use of the
muscles by causing tremor and weakness, but does not influence the functions of
the higher intellectual centers." This is a simplified statement for laymen furnished me by high medical authority.

an alertness, a curiosity, an interest in material things; a concern with books and people, the theater, politics, I had not
observed in my chats with him in the 1920's and 1930's. I
reminded him that for some years I had urged him, as others
had done, to re-establish his contact with the theater, for his
own sake and for the sake of the theater: we needed him,
possibly he needed us. Instead of repeating what he had so
often said and written, he seemed no longer to object to being
a part of the practical theater; he made no complaints about
publicity, casting, having to meet strangers. I thought I could
detect in him even a little pleasure and excitement in the
prospect of casting his new play, being on hand at rehearsals.

And even when he told me he had done no writing for
more than two years, he didn't seem too greatly concerned.
I began to feel that he was almost enjoying himself.

Then we touched on many subjects—motion pictures, the
radio, music; in particular, the popularity of the O'Neill plays
in foreign countries. He showed me the latest batch of his
plays in translation that had been sent him from Europe: a
complete set of his works, bound in full leather, from Portu-
gal; paper-bound volumes from Romania and Greece and
Russia. He told with a broad grin of the banning in Russia
of *Days Without End,* said he had been blacklisted in that
country—evidently because they thought he had become an
apologist for Catholicism.

And then he talked about *The Iceman Cometh.* He gave
me a set of proofs, and said he thought I would like the play.
"Mere physical violence—mere bigness, is not important.
You'll see that *The Iceman* is a very simple play: one set;
I've certainly observed the Unities all right, characterization,
but no plot in the ordinary sense; I didn't need plot: the
people are enough."

"About the 'big' Cycle, well, I've made lots of changes
in the scheme. I've destroyed two of the plays. I want to live
to the age of seventy; to add some more things to the Cycle
as outlined." He said that *A Touch of the Poet,* which was

scheduled for production by the Guild next season, was to have been the fifth title in the Cycle, but he had decided to detach it and have it produced separately, or at least as one of a loosely related group of plays of which *The Iceman* was to be the first and *A Moon for the Misbegotten* the second.

On Fifth Avenue, a couple of blocks away, the Irish of New York were parading: it was St. Patrick's Day, and I wondered why a man who called himself O'Neill was not marching. Again the broad grin, and when I said goodbye I couldn't help thinking that this recluse, this shy and introspective seeker after truth and beauty, this sufferer from the ills of the flesh, might indeed some day be found if not in a parade, at least on the sidelines, an anonymous spectator of the great American scene.

In early September, 1946, O'Neill gave an interview to the press. It took place at the offices of the Theatre Guild. For some reason, never made clear to me, the interviewers were reporters, and only a couple of critics were present, Rosamond Gilder of *Theatre Arts* being one of them. Also, apparently, no stenographic report was made, and I have yet found no complete record in any newspaper story. According to John S. Wilson (reporting in *PM* on Sept. 3), O'Neill looked "gaunt but tanned, his gray hair turning white at the temples . . . His hands shook nervously." Miss Gilder wanted to get things started, and made a statement that got O'Neill reminiscing, and before long he was talking about the "intent of his cycle of nine plays." The playwright elucidated his ideas as follows:

"I'm going on the theory that the United States, instead of being the most successful country in the world, is the greatest failure . . . because it was given everything, more than any other country. Through moving as rapidly as it has, it hasn't acquired any real roots. Its main idea is that everlasting game of trying to possess your own soul by the possession of something outside of it, too. America is the prime example of this because it happened so quickly and with such immense resources. This was really said in the Bible much better. We are the greatest example of 'For what shall it profit a man, if he shall gain the whole world, and lose his own soul?'·We had so much and could have gone either way . . . If the human race is so damned stupid that in two thousand years it hasn't had brains enough to appreciate that the secret of happiness is contained in one simple sentence which you'd think any grammar school kid could understand and apply, then it's time we dumped it down the nearest drain and let the ants have a chance. That simple sentence is: 'What shall it profit a man—' ' "

(O'Neill told me, a few weeks later, he had added that the same philosophy could also be found in the teachings of Buddha, Lao-Tse, even Mohammed.)

When asked about his plans for the future, he answered: "I hope to resume writing as soon as I can, but the war has thrown me completely off base and I have to get back to it again. I have to get back to a sense of writing being worthwhile. In fact, I'd have to pretend."

Miss Gilder reports, in her radio broadcast, *The American Theatre in Review* (Sept. 5), that at the same interview "a youngster" asked O'Neill, "How can one learn to be a playwright?" O'Neill "looked at his interlocutor for a long moment and then said very quietly: 'Take some wood and canvas and nails and things. Build yourself a theater, a stage, light it, learn about it. When you've done that you will probably know how to write a play—that is to say if you can.' " This, I take it, was not a flippant remark. Is it necessary to add that the experienced playwright was here advising a beginner to remember that what he has to show and say must be conveyed in terms of physical theater?

Then O'Neill was asked about his new play, *The Iceman Cometh*. What he said belongs properly in the following pages.

THE ICEMAN COMETH

MARK BARRON, one of the reporters at the mass interview, relates that the playwright said *The Iceman* is "part of an interlocking series of plays, though each is complete in itself. The second [after *The Iceman*] is *A Moon for the Misbegotten*, the third, *A Touch of the Poet*, and the fourth, *Long Day's Journey into Night*." *The Iceman*, he added, was written in 1939, and *A Moon* in 1943. At present [February 1947] the Theatre Guild plans to produce the last-named play during the current season; this is to be followed by *A Touch of the Poet*. As for *Long Day's Journey*, George Jean Nathan (writing in *The American Mercury*, October 1946) says that O'Neill will not allow it to be produced for some time to come, "for reasons which I may not yet specify." In the mass interview the author said that it would not be offered until twenty-five years after his death. "It is a real story . . . also laid in 1912. There's one person in it who is still alive." Asked whether he himself was a character in the play, he replied, "I won't tell you a word about it."

The Iceman Cometh was produced by the Theatre Guild at the Martin Beck Theater. It opened October 9, 1946. It was an imposing occasion, O'Neill's return to the theater after a twelve years' silence. The play was long, the curtain rising before five, and there was an intermission for dinner. A few weeks later the play was acted straight through without the intermission. As these lines are written the public has clearly shown that it is going to patronize the play for a long time.

The scene of *The Iceman Cometh* is the "back room and a section of the bar of Harry Hope's saloon" in the year 1912, a low dive patronized by a strange assortment of bums, male and female, most of them hopeless wrecks who find in the liquor generously furnished them by the easygoing proprietor an escape from the realities of a world in which they no longer have a place. Here are the damaged souls who in their day have sought success, honor and glory—a Boer War general, a British captain, a disillusioned anarchist, a Harvard Law School graduate, a Negro gambler, a circus man, barkeepers, streetwalkers, a youth who has betrayed his mother and the political cause that was her life. Each of these down-and-outs tries in his lucid moments to explain himself, to account for his failure, or deny it, and each is driven ultimately to forget or ignore it. Each, too, manages to sustain himself by creating some kind of illusion, some brand of besotted pipe dream. As the play opens they are anxiously awaiting the arrival of Hickey, former friend and companion of them all, a salesman who turns up periodically to give them a party. Hickey turns up on schedule and provides lavish entertainment; but he also provides, what they had not expected and certainly never wanted, a long lecture on the evils of pipe-dreaming. He has himself stopped drinking, and he claims that he has at last faced reality; not otherwise, he tells them, can they win happiness. He persuades each of his friends to begin a new "life of peace and contentment where no pipe dreaming can ever nag at you again." Having, as he thinks, found salvation for himself, he will not rest until he has sold it to the others. They must rid themselves of the "damned guilt that makes you lie to yourself you're something you're not." There is something in Hickey's eloquence that forces each sorry wreck to sober up long enough to make himself presentable, and start forth to do today what has for years been put off till tomorrow. But each in turn comes back to the saloon, miserable, disillusioned, facing an intolerable reality. Hickey's solution does not work, for instead of bringing peace and happiness it plunges each of its victims still deeper into his well of misery. But Hickey has not despaired; he will tell his friends how he had found the light, and he tells them the story of his life and how the light came to him. But he reveals more than he had intended, uncovers depths he had hardly understood himself, and his companions see that he too has had his pipe-dreams. He who had found happiness in the love of his wife, has killed her in order to save her from himself. "The last night," he confesses, "I'd driven myself crazy trying to figure some way out for her." But there was only one way, "so I killed her . . . I saw I'd always known that was the only possible way to give her peace and free her from the misery of loving me." In an access of fear, and momentarily terrified by the revelation of himself that has come from his deep probing, he denies for a second what he has just confessed: "You know I must have been insane? . . ."

But there is no way out. "Who the hell cares?" asks Hope, and as Hickey is taken off by the police, Hope eagerly accepts the explanation that everything Hickey told them, as well as his attempt to reform them, took shape in the mind of a lunatic. And the bums start drinking again, discovering at first that the whiskey has no effect on them, but as Hickey's "crazy" notions recede into the background the liquor begins to exercise its potent magic. Hickey has done what he had to do, and the wrecks he thought he was helping return to their pipe-dreams: all but the anarchist and the youth who betrayed his mother. For them there remains only self-destruction, the quick kind, a little more violent and sudden than the death awaiting the others.

There are many ways of telling the story of this play; there are varying interpretations that can be read into or thrust upon it; there are philosophical ideas that may be, and have been, drawn from it. The critics' notices of the first performance offered a wide choice of interpretations of the play's "meaning"; special articles devoted to it showed amazing differences of opinion on its "significance," or lack of significance. A good deal has been said about the symbolic "Iceman" motif, of the author's determination to preach a sermon. The truth is, I believe, that O'Neill has done many things in his play: he has preached, and he has pondered openly and directly on the destiny of man, his false hopes and ideas; and he has not hesitated to let his chief characters utter ideas that might have been more effectively suggested, merely, in terms of pure drama, and not painstakingly articulated in sentence and speeches; and he has called into his service psychological and scientific facts and beliefs that too often break or intrude upon the dramatic mood he is establishing, and that these start us thinking and sometimes confuse us. Now I don't think it necessary for the author to follow each idea that 'crops up in the course of a play to its logical conclusion, nor analyze its meaning. Nor do I think O'Neill intends that his audience shall fit together all the pieces which, when assembled, form a dramatic whole. Before all else O'Neill is a man of the theater, whose main business is to devise a play that shall stir an audience through its emotions, and only incidentally, if at all, to make it think. A great play rarely forces us to work out an intellectual problem; what we get from it is an abiding sense of basic reality, a spectacle of man grappling with life. We may, and usually do, draw our own conclusions from what we see and hear, but these conclusions are never either unclear in themselves or hard to figure out. They are oftener than not, when reduced to their essence, simple truisms that, when they are put into words, seem not worth phrasing. "Yes, that is what happens to a man who is false to his ideals"; or "Man comes to grief when he thinks he can enslave his fellowmen."

John Chapman, writing in the New York *Daily News* (Oct. 10, 1946) was one of the reviewers who gave himself up wholly to the simple job of watching *The Iceman Cometh* as a show rather than a solemn pronouncement. He says he "had a feeling . . . that some of my neighbors at the . . . premiere were so busy looking for symbolism, so intent upon finding hidden meanings, so afraid they might miss the master's message and risk being considered obtuse, that they had little time left for doing the very simple thing and the only thing an audience is supposed to do—to sit in a comfortable chair and take in a play." In another piece written for the same paper the same critic wrote (Dec. 20), "I can only report that on first hearing, it held me for every moment and there was not one instant of it that I did not relish." Even though Mr. Chapman goes on to say some very wise words on his ideas arising from the acted play, he makes it clear that his own philosophical reflections simply grew out of the spectacle he had seen, and were not what made the play a thing of joy to behold.

On the other hand, there is surely no reason why meanings, intended or not, should not be read into the play. The point I make is that there is no magic formula needed to enable you to understand what O'Neill is talking about. If a play requires that kind of explanation very likely it is not worth seeing. But if, allowing yourself to enjoy *The Iceman* as a play and not as a psychological and philosophical document, you can at the same time (or later) relate yourself and your own problems to it, you may get out of it some added element. If so, so much the better. For example, Rosamond Gilder, writing in the December, 1946, issue of *Theatre Arts,* was able, while enjoying the play as a show, to summarize the author's ideas more articulately, and I think more accurately, than any other of her fellow critics. She writes: ". . . it is through Hickey who has known the love that passeth understanding and has rejected it that we glimpse O'Neill's ultimate meaning. Blind, besotted and misguided, man haunted by death lives by lies. 'The lie of a pipe dream is what gives life to the whole misbegotten mad lot of us, drunk or sober,' Larry says at the opening of the play. But there is a truth which is not the truth of alcohol or political shibboleths, or psychology or philosophy, or even the truth of 'facing the truth,' which Hickey preaches. The greatest illusion of all is to believe that disillusionment—the unaided processes of the intellect—can solve man's dilemma. There is a force that, like the love that Hickey's wife bore him, is made of understanding and forgiveness. Man finds such love intolerable. 'I couldn't forgive her for forgiving me,' Hickey explains. 'I caught myself hating her for making me hate myself so much.' There is a limit to the guilt you can feel and the forgiveness and pity you can take. And so man denies, destroys and blasphemes such love, only in the end to find that this too will be forgiven. The denizens of Hickey's world and of the world at large find a simple answer to Hickey's final revelation. The man is mad! Hamlet to the contrary notwithstanding, there is nothing more in heaven and earth than can be compassed in any current philosophy. Pass the bottle. Drink up. What the hell! It's a good play, brother, why bother."

And this is another way of looking at the matter. And a good one. Incidentally, the points Miss Gilder raises will suggest how the same O'Neill who tried to say too much, and too literally, in *Days Without End*, was still busy fitting into his intellectual scheme of things the baffling problem of man and his destiny; our thoughts go back to *Dynamo*, the play that showed man worshiping science and seeking from it an answer to his unending quest for certitude. But I see no reason at this time to attempt to follow, as so many of the O'Neill "heroes" have tried to do, the development of this idea or that in the plays we have so far considered in our study. Of the intrinsic value of these ideas I am by no means certain; of their value as means to an end, "end" here meaning the plays as they appear in our theater, there can be no question.

IN MID-CAREER

EUGENE O'NEILL is a little over fifty-eight. He has been writing plays almost uninterruptedly for more than thirty years; in spite of ill-health he probably spends more time every year at his work than any other living playwright. He has today a firmer grasp of the technical problems of his craft than he ever had; *The Iceman Cometh* and *A Moon for the Misbegotten*, the only plays I have seen from his latest period, show to a marked degree the man's skill in creating sound drama that will hold and interest audiences; his dialogue in these two works is more fully rounded, less "literary," in all ways more satisfactory than in any of his other plays, with the possible exception of *Mourning Becomes Electra.*

My talk with him in March left me feeling that, even though he had not written a play for over two years, he had by no means lost interest in planning new works. On the contrary, his mind, I think, was more active than ever, his curiosity about the world more acute, his concern about men and their affairs more noticeable. An interviewer notes in May that he "has been seeing prizefights and baseball games."

He expressed no dread to me of the forthcoming rehearsals for *The Iceman Cometh;* I believe he was even a little excited over the prospect; in discussing his casting problems he showed a wide knowledge of actors surprising in a man who rarely goes to the theater and had not been near Broadway for many years.

There is an interesting passage in S. J. Woolf's article, *Eugene O'Neill Returns After Twelve Years,* in the New York *Times* of Sept. 15, 1946, where O'Neill explains in detail his feeling about actors in his own plays. He says that except in the case of Charles Gilpin in *The Emperor Jones* no actor ever carried "every notion of a character I had in mind. . . . I am not saying that some of the actors and actresses who interpreted my plays did not add something to them. But, after all, even an owl thinks her owlets are the most beautiful babies in the world and that's the way an author feels about his stage children. It is for this reason that I always attend the rehearsals of my plays. While I do not want to change the personalities of the artists acting in them, I want to make it clear to them what was in my mind when I wrote the play."

It was after *The Iceman Cometh* had opened in New York that I went to see him again. That was about the middle of November. He and Mrs. O'Neill were comfortably settled in the penthouse apartment where Edward Sheldon had lived for many years. The place was well furnished, filled with the O'Neills' books and phonograph records, and it looked like home. The O'Neill who greeted me at the door and showed me around the place was not the semi-invalid I had seen last March; he looked much healthier, he spoke more fluently, he was patient with my small-talk—about new plays, the radio, motion pictures, the high cost of living; we even exchanged views on the upbringing of our children. We did indeed talk shop, and he spoke at some length about *The Iceman,* how he had found a talented young actor in the cast, who understudied one of the major roles; how he had had to change the business at the end of the play because few if any of the cast could sing, and how he had made some cuts in the dialogue.

When I mentioned the mass interview I said I got the impression that he didn't very much mind the ordeal, and he smiled in assent. Of course, what he had said was not fully reported, but then he didn't expect that.

About his new plays, he described how he had recently discarded one act of *A Touch of the Poet* and written another. The script was not yet in shape and he didn't have a copy to show me at the time. But if I wanted to read *A Moon for the Misbegotten,* that was practically ready for rehearsal. One thing he had to do, though, and that was to make minor changes in one of the principal roles. "He's a young man (the play's set in 1912), son of a prominent actor, and people might think it was myself, which it isn't."

I looked at some of the books that lined the walls in the living-room, and wondered why there were so many about Robespierre. Ten or a dozen in all. "I did a lot of reading about him, in English—I don't read French easily. Robespierre sums it all up: the idealist at first, the righteous man; he gets power; he uses it; he misuses it; tragedy. The perfect pattern, you see."

"Are you going to write a play about him?"

"Well, I was thinking about it for a time."

I didn't follow this up. Perhaps he will, after he finishes the big Cycle, after he reaches the age of seventy. This is not what he said, but I would not be surprised if he did.

A MOON FOR THE MISBEGOTTEN

I READ the typescript the next day. It is, as O'Neill had described it to me, a simple play that begins as farce and ends as tragedy. Yet tragedy is not the word, since one of the two principal characters emerges from her experience with a heightened sense of spiritual completeness. There is exaltation in this love story, and an inescapable feeling of joy; it is alive and moving, and its lyric mood is a positive thing. The play has not yet been produced and I have no right at this time to outline its plot beyond saying that it is about a large and lusty Irish farm girl who has none of the obvious trappings of conventional beauty, and an attractive but disillusioned and dissipated man, who fall in love with each other, and part soon after.

The play was announced for production by the Theatre Guild and was to have been seen in New York in the late fall of 1946. But there have been casting problems, and O'Neill's latest report on the matter is that they can't find the right director: those under consideration have Hollywood contracts. I asked him the other day why he didn't direct the play himself. "The trouble is I can tell the actors what to do but they won't do it."

In 1936 I added a few pages to my book under a caption recklessly called "The Future." Among other things I said that there seemed to be no limit to his ambition, and I quoted something he told me about his plans a few years before. "All the most dramatic episodes of my life," he said, "I have so far kept out of my plays, and most of the things I have seen happen to other people. I've hardly begun to work up all this material, but I'm saving up a lot of it for one thing in particular, a cycle of plays I hope to do some day. There'll be nine separate plays, to be acted on nine successive nights; together they will form a sort of dramatic autobiography, something in the style of *War and Peace* or *Jean-Christophe*."

And I went on to quote a statement of O'Neill's made in 1922, which seemed to me, except for the last sentence, as apt as it was when first uttered; I am now quoting it again: "I intend to use whatever I can make my own, to write about anything under the sun in any manner that fits or can be invented to fit the subject. And I shall never be influenced by any consideration but one: Is it the truth as I know it— or, better still, feel it? If so, shoot, and let the splinters fly wherever they may. If not, not. This sounds brave and bold —but it isn't. It simply means that I want to do what gives me pleasure and worth in my own eyes, and don't care to do what doesn't . . . It is just life that interests me as a thing in itself. The why and wherefore I haven't attempted to touch on yet."

Even before 1936 he had of course attempted the why and wherefore, and in so doing he has, I am convinced, occasionally involved himself overmuch with explanations, when revelation would have proved more moving, and in the final analysis more convincing in the theater. Yet, with undiminished vigor and an enormous curiosity about mankind, he goes on his single-minded way. He has written a good deal that is already forgotten, and that is just as well; he has given us plays that are inept and over-violent, some plays that are pretentious; he has too often striven to write jewelled passages of prose instead of stinging dialogue; he is, and always was, a maker of plays that are good, bad, and indifferent. He has written a few that stand high among the noble achievements of the poets who have made the theater, at its best, an instrument of joy and consolation. In a word, he is a man whose achievements have never quite measured up to his aims. But then, whose have?

The subject of this book is alive and vigorous; he is not ready to retire either from the theater or the world of men. These concluding sentences are written not two hours after I talked with O'Neill over the telephone; he told me what he had been working at and what he planned to do about the casting of his new play. But this record must come to a close. The close, as O'Neill said many years ago about the end of one of his plays, is only a comma. I feel surer of the man's future today than I did when twenty years ago I brought the first embryonic version of this book to its tentative conclusion.

First Productions of Plays

Bound East for Cardiff. Provincetown Players.[1] Wharf Theater, Provincetown, Mass., 2nd bill, summer, 1916.

Thirst. Provincetown Players. Wharf Theater, Provincetown, Mass., 4th bill, summer, 1916.

Before Breakfast. Provincetown Players. The Playwrights' Theater, Macdougal St., New York, Dec. 1, 1916.

Fog. Provincetown Players. The Playwrights' Theater, Macdougal St., New York, Jan., 1917.

The Sniper. Provincetown Players. The Playwrights' Theater, Macdougal St., New York, Feb. 16, 1917.

In the Zone. Washington Square Players. Comedy Theater, New York, Oct. 31, 1917.

The Long Voyage Home. Provincetown Players. The Playwrights' Theater, Macdougal St., New York, Nov. 2, 1917.

'Ile. Provincetown Players. The Playwrights' Theater, Macdougal St., New York, Nov. 30, 1917.

The Rope. Provincetown Players. The Playwrights' Theater, Macdougal St., New York, April 26, 1918.

Where the Cross is Made. Provincetown Players. The Playwrights' Theater, Macdougal St., New York, Nov. 22, 1918.

The Moon of the Caribbees. Provincetown Players. The Playwrights' Theater, Macdougal St., New York, Dec. 20, 1918.

The Dreamy Kid. Provincetown Players. The Playwrights' Theater, Macdougal St., New York, Oct. 31, 1919.

Beyond the Horizon. Produced by John D. Williams, Morosco Theater, New York, Feb. 2, 1920.

Chris Christopherson. Produced by George C. Tyler. Atlantic City, March 8, 1920.

Exorcism. Provincetown Players. The Playwrights' Theater, Macdougal St., New York, March 26, 1920.

The Emperor Jones. Provincetown Players. The Playwrights' Theater, Macdougal St., New York, Nov. 3, 1920.

[1] I.e., the group that was known by that name in the fall of 1916.

DIFF'RENT. Provincetown Players. The Playwrights' Theater, Macdougal St., New York, Dec. 27, 1920.

GOLD. Produced by John D. Williams. Frazee Theater, New York, June 1, 1921.

ANNA CHRISTIE. Produced by Arthur Hopkins. Vanderbilt Theater, New York, Nov. 2, 1921.

THE STRAW. Produced by George C. Tyler. Greenwich Village Theater, New York, Nov. 10, 1921.

THE FIRST MAN. Produced at the Neighborhood Playhouse, direction of Augustin Duncan, New York, March 4, 1922.

THE HAIRY APE. Provincetown Players. The Playwrights' Theater, Macdougal St., New York, March 9, 1922.

WELDED. Produced by Macgowan, Jones and O'Neill in association with the Selwyns. 39th St. Theater, New York, March 17, 1924.

THE ANCIENT MARINER. Produced by the Provincetown Playhouse, Inc., Provincetown Playhouse, Macdougal St., New York, April 6, 1924.

ALL GOD'S CHILLUN GOT WINGS. Produced by the Provincetown Playhouse, Inc., Provincetown Playhouse, Macdougal St., New York, May 15, 1924.

S.S. GLENCAIRN. Produced by The Barnstormers. The Barnstormers' Barn, Provincetown, Mass., Aug. 14, 1924.

DESIRE UNDER THE ELMS. Produced by the Provincetown Playhouse, Inc. Greenwich Village Theater, New York, Nov. 11, 1924.

THE FOUNTAIN. Produced by Macgowan, Jones, and O'Neill in association with A. L. Jones and Morris Green. Greenwich Village Theater, New York, Dec. 10, 1925.

THE GREAT GOD BROWN. Produced by Macgowan, Jones, and O'Neill. The Greenwich Village Theater, New York, Jan. 23, 1926.

MARCO MILLIONS. Produced by the Theater Guild. The Guild Theater, New York, Jan. 9, 1928.

STRANGE INTERLUDE. Produced by the Theater Guild. The John Golden Theater, New York, Jan. 30, 1928.

LAZARUS LAUGHED. Produced by the Pasadena Community Playhouse. The Pasadena Community Playhouse, Pasadena, Calif., April 9, 1928.

DYNAMO. Produced by the Theater Guild. The Martin Beck Theater, New York, Feb. 11, 1929.

MOURNING BECOMES ELECTRA. (A trilogy: *Homecoming, The Hunted,* and *The Haunted.*) Produced by the Theater Guild. The Guild Theater, New York, Oct. 26, 1931.

AH, WILDERNESS! Produced by the Theater Guild, Inc. Guild Theater, New York, Oct. 2, 1933.

DAYS WITHOUT END. Produced by the Theater Guild, Inc. Guild Theater, New York, Jan. 8, 1934.

THE ICEMAN COMETH. Produced by the Theater Guild, Inc. Martin Beck Theater, New York, Sept. 2, 1946.

CHECK-LIST OF THE FIRST PUBLICATION OF THE PLAYS OF EUGENE O'NEILL

(Listed in chronological order of publication)

BY RALPH SANBORN

The plays and all other works by Eugene O'Neill—if published prior to 1931—are fully listed and collated in "A Bibliography of The Works of Eugene O'Neill," by Ralph Sanborn and Barrett H. Clark, published by Random House, New York, 1931, in a limited edition of 500 copies.

1. 1914. THIRST. American Dramatists Series. Boston, The Gorham Press. A play in one act. It also contains the first publication of these one-act plays: THE WEB, WARNINGS, FOG, and RECKLESSNESS. 12 mo. Bound in boards.

2. 1916. BOUND EAST FOR CARDIFF. The Provincetown Plays. First Series. New York, Frank Shay. It also contains "The Game" by Louise Bryant and "King Arthur's Socks" by Floyd Dell. All are plays in one act. 12 mo. Bound in paper.

3. 1916. BEFORE BREAKFAST. The Provincetown Plays. Third Series. New York, Frank Shay. It also contains "The Two Sons" by Neith Boyce and "Lima

Beans" by Alfred Kreymborg. All are plays in one
act. 12 mo. Bound in paper.

4. 1917.   THE LONG VOYAGE HOME. The *Smart Set* Magazine,
issue for October 1917. New York. A play in one
act. 8 vo. Bound in paper.

5. 1918.   'ILE. The *Smart Set* Magazine, issue for May 1918. New
York. A play in one act. 8 vo. Bound in paper.

6. 1918.   THE MOON OF THE CARIBBEES. The *Smart Set* Magazine, issue for August 1918. New York. A play in
one act. 8 vo. Bound in paper.

7. 1919.   THE MOON OF THE CARIBBEES. New York, Boni and
Liveright. It contains the first publication of IN
THE ZONE, WHERE THE CROSS IS MADE, and THE
ROPE in addition to revised texts of THE MOON
OF THE CARIBBEES, THE LONG VOYAGE HOME
and 'ILE. All are plays in one act. 12 mo. Bound in
boards.

8. 1920.   THE DREAMY KID. *Theatre Arts* Magazine, issue for
January 1920. New York. A play in one act. 8 vo.
Bound in paper.

9. 1920.   BEYOND THE HORIZON. New York, Boni and Liveright.
A play in three acts. 12 mo. Bound in boards.

10. 1921.   THE EMPEROR JONES. *Theatre Arts* Magazine, issue
for January 1921. A play in eight scenes. 8 vo.
Bound in paper.

11. 1921.   THE EMPEROR JONES, DIFF'RENT, THE STRAW. New
York, Boni and Liveright. It also contains the first
publication of DIFF'RENT, a play in two acts, and
THE STRAW, a play in three acts. 12 mo. Bound
in boards.

12. 1921.   GOLD. New York, Boni and Liveright. A play in four
acts. 12 mo. Bound in boards.

13. 1922.   THE HAIRY APE, ANNA CHRISTIE, THE FIRST MAN.
New York, Boni and Liveright. The first is a play
in eight scenes, and the others are plays in four
acts. 12 mo. Bound in boards.

14. 1924.   ALL GOD'S CHILLUN GOT WINGS. The *American
Mercury* Magazine, issue for February 1924. New
York. A play in two acts. 8 vo. Bound in paper.

15. 1924. ALL GOD'S CHILLUN GOT WINGS, WELDED. New York, Boni and Liveright. It also contains the first publication of WELDED, a play in three acts. 12 mo. Bound in boards.

16. 1925. DESIRE UNDER THE ELMS. "Complete Works of Eugene O'Neill." Two Volumes. Limited Edition of 1200 sets. New York, Boni and Liveright. Volume II contains the first publication of DESIRE UNDER THE ELMS. A play in three parts. 8 vo. Bound in boards.

17. 1926. THE GREAT GOD BROWN, THE FOUNTAIN. New York, Boni and Liveright. The former is a play in four acts with a prologue and an epilogue. The latter is a play in three parts. 8 vo. Bound in cloth.

18. 1927. MARCO MILLIONS. New York, Boni and Liveright. A play in three acts with a prologue and an epilogue. 8 vo. Bound in cloth.

19. 1927. LAZARUS LAUGHED. New York, Boni and Liveright. A play in four acts. 8 vo. Bound in cloth.

20. 1928. STRANGE INTERLUDE. New York, Boni and Liveright. A play in nine acts. 8 vo. Bound in cloth.

21. 1929. DYNAMO. New York, Horace Liveright. A play in three acts. 8 vo. Bound in cloth.

22. 1931. MOURNING BECOMES ELECTRA. New York, Horace Liveright, Inc. A trilogy in which Part One has four acts, Part Two has five acts and Part Three has four acts. 8 vo. Bound in cloth.

23. 1933. AH, WILDERNESS! New York, Random House. A play in four acts. 8 vo. Bound in cloth.

24. 1934. DAYS WITHOUT END. New York, Random House. A play in four acts. 8 vo. Bound in cloth.

25. 1946. THE ICEMAN COMETH. New York, Random House. A play in four acts. 8 vo. Bound in cloth.

An Alphabetical Index List of Published Plays

The number shown beside each play indicates the item in the foregoing numbered CHECK-LIST where the first publication of that play is to be found.

Ah, Wilderness!—23

All God's Chillun Got Wings—14

Anna Christie—13

Before Breakfast—3

Beyond the Horizon—9

Bound East for Cardiff—2

Days Without End—24

Desire Under the Elms—16

Diff'rent—11

Dynamo—21

Fog—1

Gold—12

'Ile—5

In the Zone—7

Lazarus Laughed—20

Marco Millions—18

Mourning Becomes Electra—22

Recklessness—1

Strange Interlude—20

The Dreamy Kid—8

The Emperor Jones—10

The First Man—13

The Fountain—17

The Great God Brown—17

The Hairy Ape—13

The Iceman Cometh—25

The Long Voyage Home—4

The Moon of the Caribbees—6

The Rope—7

The Straw—11

The Web—1

Thirst—1

Warnings—1

Welded—15

Where the Cross Is Made—7

The above Check-List covers only first printings of the O'Neill plays. There have been many editions of the single plays published, some editions in which two or more plays were issued, several low-priced volumes and some expensive limited series. At the present time the most convenient edition, one that is likely to be kept in print, is the set of three volumes,

The Plays of Eugene O'Neill, issued by Random House. This includes all the published plays except those in the *Thirst* volume, and *The Iceman Cometh*, which has recently been issued separately by Random House.

Letters, Articles, Notes, etc., by O'Neill

List of Published Material

O'Neill's published verse in the New London Telegraph and elsewhere is referred to on pp. 44-45 of this volume. All this, as well as all the other identified verse, is reprinted in A Bibliography of the Works of Eugene O'Neill, *by Ralph Sanborn and Barrett H. Clark, New York, 1931.*

Tomorrow [a story]. In *The Seven Arts* [a magazine], New York, Vol. 2, No. 8. June 1917.

A Letter "From Eugene O'Neill" [Provincetown, Dec. 12, 1921, on *Anna Christie*], New York *Times*, Dec. 16, 1921.

A Letter From O'Neill, New York *Times*, April 11, 1920.

Strindberg and Our Theater, Provincetown Playbill, No. 1, Season, 1923–24.

Are the Actors to Blame? Provincetown Playbill, No. 1, Season, 1925–26.

Note in the program of *The Fountain*, Greenwich Playbill, No. 3, Season 1925–26.

A series of letters to George Jean Nathan. In Isaac Goldberg's article, *Playwright and Critic: The Record of a Stimulating Correspondence*, Boston *Evening Transcript*, Oct. 31, 1925. These are reprinted in Goldberg's *The Theatre of George Jean Nathan*, New York, 1927.

Eugene O'Neill Writes About His Latest Play, "The Great God Brown" [also under other titles in other New York papers of next day. A letter to the press], New York *Evening Post*, Feb. 13, 1926.

O'Neill Talks About "Beyond the Horizon," New York *Evening Post*, Nov. 27, 1926.

Anathema! Litanies of Negation. By Benjamin De Casseres. With a Foreword by Eugene O'Neill. New York, Gotham Book Mart, 1928.

O'Neill's Own Story of "Electra" in the Making, New York *Herald Tribune,* Nov. 3, 1931.

Memoranda on Masks. In *The American Spectator,* New York, Nov. 1932.

Notes on each of the plays in *The Complete Plays of Eugene O'Neill. Wilderness Edition.* 12 vols. New York, 1935.

Prof. G. P. Baker, A Note and Some Communications. In *George Pierce Baker, A Memorial.* New York, 1939.

SELECTED READING LIST

The following list of references is based largely on the author's collection of basic materials. It is not complete, but it does include a large part of the books, articles, bibliographies, and scattered data which offer original material on the subject and specific or general summaries of O'Neill's work. It should be noted that few items are listed for the past fifteen years. This is because the majority of the summaries and biographical articles after 1930 are based on the earlier sources here mentioned, the writers customarily lifting such facts without giving proper credit. Reviews of individual plays in periodicals are not mentioned, nor are chapters or sections in books on the drama and theater, except for a few standard reference works and those containing a certain amount of source material.

BOOKS

Mantle, Burns. *The Best Plays of 1919–20 and the Year Book of the Drama in America.* Boston, 1920. (Same title except for dates. Boston through 1925, thereafter New York, to date. Each volume lists and describes each O'Neill play that appeared during the current year.)

American Playwrights of Today. N. Y., 1929.

Contemporary American Playwrights. N. Y., 1938.

Nathan, George Jean. *Comedians All.* N. Y., 1919.

The Theatre, The Drama, The Girl. N. Y., 1921.

The World in Falseface. N. Y., 1923.

Materia Critica. N. Y., 1924.

The Autobiography of an Attitude. N. Y., 1925.

The House of Satan. N. Y., 1926.

Art of the Night. N. Y., 1928.

The Testament of a Critic. N. Y., 1931.

The Intimate Notebooks of George Jean Nathan. N. Y., 1932.

Passing Judgments. N. Y., 1935.

The Theatre of the Moment. N. Y., 1936.

Encyclopedia of the Theatre. N. Y., 1940.

The Entertainment of a Nation. N. Y., 1942.

Hamilton, Clayton. *Seen on the Stage.* N. Y., 1920.

Conversations on Contemporary Drama. N. Y., 1924.

Macgowan, Kenneth, *The Theatre of Tomorrow.* N. Y., 1921.

Goldberg, Isaac. *The Drama of Transition.* Cincinnati, 1922.

The Theatre of George Jean Nathan. N. Y., 1926.

Schelling, Felix E. *Appraisements and Asperities.* Philadelphia, 1922.

Woollcott, Alexander. *Shouts and Murmurs.* N. Y., 1922.

Enchanted Aisles. N. Y., 1924.

Sayler, Oliver M. *Our American Theatre.* N. Y., 1923.

Boyd, Ernest. *Portraits: Real and Imaginary.* N. Y., 1924.

Boynton, Percy H. *Some Contemporary Americans.* Chicago, 1924.

Sutton, Graham. *Some Contemporary Dramatists.* N. Y., 1924.

Cheney, Sheldon. *The Art Theatre.* N. Y., 1925.

Dickinson, Thomas H. *Dramatists of the New American Theatre.* N. Y., 1925.

Kenton, Edna. *Preface to Greek Coins of George Cram Cook.* N. Y., 1925.

Kreymborg, Alfred. *Troubadour.* N. Y., 1925.

Moses, Montrose J. *The American Dramatist.* Boston, 1925.

Clark, Barrett H. *Eugene O'Neill.* N. Y., 1926.

(Same, revised and rewritten as *Eugene O'Neill, the Man and His Plays.* N. Y., 1929, 1933, 1936.)

A Study of the Modern Drama. N. Y., 1925.

(Same, revised, 1938.)

An Hour of American Drama. Philadelphia, 1930.

Glaspell, Susan. *The Road to the Temple.* N. Y., 1927.

Quinn, Arthur Hobson. *A History of the American Drama from the Civil War to the Present Day.* Vol. 2. N. Y., 1927.

Sargent, Elizabeth S. *Fire Under the Andes.* N. Y., 1927.

Karsner, David. *Sixteen Authors to One.* N. Y., 1928.

Whipple, T. K. *Spokesmen.* N. Y., 1928.

Eaton, Walter Prichard. *The Theatre Guild.* N. Y., 1929.
  The Drama in English. N. Y., 1930.

Manly, John M., and Rickert, Edith. *Contemporary American Literature.* Rev. ed. N. Y., 1929.

Skolsky, Sidney. *Times Square Tintypes.* N. Y., 1930.

Mickle, Alan D. *Six Plays of Eugene O'Neill.* N. Y., 1929.

Brown, John Mason. *Upstage.* N. Y., 1930.
  The Modern Theater in Revolt. N. Y., 1929.
  Letters from Greenroom Ghosts. N. Y., 1934.
  Deutsch, Helen, and Hanau, Stella. *The Provincetown; A Story of the Theatre.* N. Y., 1931.

Sanborn, Ralph, and Clark, Barrett H. *A Bibliography of the Works of Eugene O'Neill.* N. Y., 1931.

Winther, Sophus Keith. *Eugene O'Neill: A Critical Study.* N. Y., 1934.

Halline, Allan Gates. *American Plays, Selected and Edited with Critical Introductions and Bibliographies.* N. Y., 1935.

Skinner, Richard Dana. *Eugene O'Neill, a Poet's Quest.* N. Y., 1935.

Lawson, John Howard. *Theory and Technique of Playwriting.* N. Y., 1936.

Flexner, Eleanor. *American Playwrights: 1918–1938.* N. Y., 1938.

Block, Anita. *The Changing World in Plays and Theatre.* N. Y., 1939.

Krutch, Joseph Wood. *The American Drama Since 1918.* N. Y., 1939.

O'Hara, Frank H. *Today in American Drama.* Chicago, 1939.

Gorelik, Mordecai. *New Theatres for Old.* N. Y., 1940.

ARTICLES AND PAMPHLETS

Clark, Barrett H. Eugene O'Neill. *Theatre Arts Monthly.* N. Y., May 1926.
  The Plays of Eugene G. O'Neill. *Sun.* N. Y., May 18, 1919.
  A New American Dramatist. *Arts Gazette.* London, May 1920.
  The Real Background of O'Neill in His "S.S. Glencairn" Group. *Herald Tribune.* N. Y., Feb. 10, 1929.

Coleman, Alta M. Personality Portraits—Eugene O'Neill. *The Theatre,* April 1920.

Woollcott, Alexander. The Rise of Eugene O'Neill. *Everybody's Magazine.* N. Y., June 1920.

Eaton, Walter Prichard. Eugene O'Neill. *Theatre Arts Magazine.* N. Y., Oct. 1920.

The American Drama Flowers—Eugene O'Neill as a Great Playwright. *World's Work.* N. Y., Nov. 1926.

Eugene O'Neill as a Great Playwright. *World Today.* N. Y., 1927.

The Hermit of Cape Cod. *Herald Tribune.* N. Y., Jan. 8, 1928.

Sayler, Oliver M. The Work of Eugene O'Neill. *The Drama.* Chicago, March 1921.

The Real Eugene O'Neill. *Century Magazine.* N. Y., Jan. 1922.

Loving, Pierre. Enter Eugene O'Neill. *Bookman.* N. Y., Aug. 1921.

Crawford, Jack R. A Broadway Philosopher. *The Drama.* Chicago, Jan. 1921.

Mollan, Malcolm. Making Plays with a Tragic End. An Intimate Interview with Eugene O'Neill Who Tells Why He Does It. *Public Ledger.* Philadelphia, Jan. 22, 1922.

Lewisohn, Ludwig. The Development of Eugene O'Neill. *The Nation.* N. Y., March 22, 1922.

Macgowan, Kenneth. The Theatrical Callboard. *Vanity Fair.* N. Y., April 1922.

Eugene O'Neill as a Realist. *Times.* N. Y., March 23, 1924.

O'Neill in His Own Plays. *Times.* N. Y., Jan. 2, 1927.

Mullett, Mary B. The Extraordinary Story of Eugene O'Neill. *American Magazine.* N. Y., Nov. 1922.

Young, Stark. An Estimate of Eugene O'Neill. *New Republic.* N. Y., Nov. 15, 1922.

O'Neill, J. F. What a Sanatorium Did for Eugene O'Neill. *Journal of Outdoor Life.* N. Y., June 1923.

Breese, J. M. Home on the Dunes. *Country Life in America.* N. Y., Nov. 1923.

Bird, Carol. Eugene O'Neill—The Inner Man. *Theatre Magazine.* N. Y., June 1924.

Sweeney, Charles P. Back to the Source of Plays Written by Eugene O'Neill. *World.* N. Y., Nov. 9, 1924.

Kalodyme, Louis. O'Neill Lifts the Curtain on His Early Days. *Times*. N. Y., Dec. 21, 1924.

Vernon, Grenville. Our Native Dramatist Comes Into His Own—Eugene O'Neill. *Theatre Magazine*. N. Y., May 1925.

Kantor, Louis. Eugene O'Neill, Able Seaman. *Princetown Playbill*, No. 2. N. Y., Season 1924–25.

Atkinson, J. Brooks. New O'Neill Aspects. *Times*. N. Y., Dec. 20, 1925.

Ibsen and O'Neill. *Times*. N. Y., Jan. 31, 1926.

Honor Enough for Everybody. *Times*. N. Y., Jan. 27, 1929.

Concluding a Dramatic Cycle. *Times*. N. Y., Feb. 17, 1929.

O'Neill Off Duty. *Times*. N. Y., Oct. 8, 1933.

Weaver, John V. A. I Knew Him When—. *World*. N. Y., Feb. 21, 1926.

Baker, George Pierce. O'Neill's First Decade. *Yale Review*. New Haven, July 1926.

Karsner, David. Eugene O'Neill at Close Range in Maine. *Herald Tribune*. N. Y., Aug. 8, 1926.

Anonymous. The Theater of Eugene O'Neill. (List of plays, including Mss lost or destroyed.) *Greenwich Playbill* (Program of The Fountain), No. 3, Season 1925–26.

Casseres, Benjamin de. How Eugene O'Neill Came Out of the Depths. *Literary Digest*. N. Y., Nov. 1926.

Eugene O'Neill, A Vignette. *Popular Biography*. N. Y., April 1930.

White, A. F. The Plays of Eugene O'Neill. In *Studies by Members of the Faculty*, Vol. 26, Western Reserve University. Cleveland, 1927.

Anonymous. A Eugene O'Neill Medley. *Sun*. N. Y., Jan. 12, 1928.

Watts, Richard, Jr. Realism Doomed, O'Neill Believes. *Herald Tribune*. N. Y., Feb. 5, 1928.

Gabriel, Gilbert. The Newer O'Neill. *Vanity Fair*. N. Y., April 1928.

Katzin, Winifred. The Great God O'Neill. *The Bookman*. N. Y., Sept. 1928.

Shipley, Joseph T. The Art of Eugene O'Neill. Seattle, Washington, 1928.

Kemp, Harry. Out of Provincetown. *Theatre Magazine*. N. Y., April 1930.

Vorse, Mary Heaton. Eugene O'Neill's Pet Saloon Is Gone. *World*. N. Y., May 4, 1930.

Morehouse, Ward. The Boulevards After Dark. *Sun*. N. Y., May 14, 1930.

Friedman, Stanley S. O'Neill Gives Advance Notice of His New Play. *Press*. Cleveland, June 14, 1930.

Ferguson, Francis. Eugene O'Neill. *Hound and Horn*. Portland, Me., Winter, 1930.

Pasley, Fred. Odyssey of Eugene O'Neill—the Ulysses of the Drama. *The News*. N. Y., Jan. 24-30 incl., 1932.

Geddes, Virgil. The Melodramadness of Eugene O'Neill. Brookfield, Conn., 1934.

Sylvester, Robert. O'Neill Sets Aside Drama for Staging 25 Years After Death. *Daily News*. N. Y., June 20, 1946.

Nathan, George Jean. Eugene O'Neill Discourses on Dramatic Art. *Journal-American*. N. Y., Aug. 22, 1946.

Anonymous. Broadway Report: O'Neill on the World and "The Iceman." (Mass interview.) *PM*. N. Y., Sept. 3, 1946.

Woolf, S. J. Eugene O'Neill Returns After Twelve Years. *Times Magazine*. N. Y., Sept. 15, 1946.

Schriftgiesser, Karl. The Iceman Cometh. *Times*. N. Y., Oct. 6, 1946.

Prideaux, Tom. Eugene O'Neill. *Life*. N. Y., Oct. 14, 1946.

Anonymous. The Ordeal of Eugene O'Neill. *Time*. N. Y., Oct. 21, 1946.

ADDENDA: 1947–1966

First Production of Plays

A Moon for the Misbegotten. Produced by the Theater Guild. Hartman Theater, Columbus, Ohio, Feb. 20, 1947.

Long Day's Journey into Night. Produced by the Royal Dramatic Theater, Stockholm, Sweden, Feb. 10, 1956. First American production at the Helen Hayes Theater, New York, Nov. 7, 1956.

A Touch of the Poet. Produced by the Royal Dramatic Theater, Stockholm, Sweden, March 29, 1957. First American production at the Helen Hayes Theater, New York, Oct. 2, 1958.

Hughie. Produced by the Royal Dramatic Theater, Stockholm, Sweden, Sept. 18, 1958. First American production at the Royale Theater, New York, Nov. 22, 1964.

Abortion. Produced at the Key Theater, St. Mark's Place, New York, Oct. 27, 1959.

The Movie Man. Produced at the Key Theater, St. Mark's Place, New York, Oct. 27, 1959.

Servitude. Produced at the Skylark Theater, New York International Airport, April 22, 1960.

First Publication of Plays

26. 1950. Abortion. *The Lost Plays*. New York, New Fathoms, 1950. (Reissued by the Citadel Press in 1958). A play in one act. 8 vo. Bound in cloth.

27. 1950. The Movie Man. *The Lost Plays*. New York, New Fathoms, 1950. (Reissued by the Citadel Press in 1958). A play in one act. 8 vo. Bound in cloth.

178

28. 1950. SERVITUDE. *The Lost Plays*. New York, New Fathoms, 1950. (Reissued by the Citadel Press in 1958. A play in three acts. 8 vo. Bound in cloth.

29. 1950. A WIFE FOR A LIFE. *The Lost Plays*. New York, New Fathoms, 1950. (Reissued by the Citadel Press in 1958). A play in one act. 8 vo. Bound in cloth.

30. 1952. A MOON FOR THE MISBEGOTTEN. New York, Random House, 1952. A play in four acts. 8 vo. Bound in cloth.

31. 1956. LONG DAY'S JOURNEY INTO NIGHT. New Haven, Yale University Press, 1956. A play in four acts. 12 mo. Bound in cloth.

32. 1957. A TOUCH OF THE POET. New Haven, Yale University Press, 1957. A play in four acts. 8 vo. Bound in paper.

33. 1959. HUGHIE. New Haven, Yale University Press, 1959. A play in one act. 12 mo.

34. 1964. MORE STATELY MANSIONS. New Haven, Yale University Press, 1964. Shortened from the author's partly revised script by Karl Ragnar Gierow and edited by Donald Gallup. A play in three acts. 12 mo. Bound in cloth and paper.

INDEX

Abortion, 49, 54

Aeschylus, 125, 126, 128, 129, 130, 131, 132, 133, 134

Agamemnon, 124, 129

Ah, Wilderness!, 137, 138, 139, 143, 149

All God's Chillun Got Wings, 93, 94, 95, 96, 99

Allen, Viola, 14

Also Sprach Zarathustra, 25

American Academy of Arts and Sciences, 39

American Magazine, 41, 85

American Mercury, 108, 154

American Spectator, 103

American Theatre in Review, The, 153

Ames, Winthrop, 108

Anatol, 65

Ancient Mariner, The, 102, 103

Anna Christie, 16, 38, 69, 75, 76, 77, 78, 79

Atkinson, J. Brooks, 102, 121

Atrocity, 54

Badger, R. G., 33

Baker, George Pierce, 9, 11, 25, 27, 28, 36, 54, 67

Ballantine, Edward J., 9, 29

Balzac, Honoré de, 61, 136

Barberá, Manuel, v

Barron, Mark, 154

Before Breakfast, 35, 37, 54, 63, 64

Belasco, David, 108

Belshazzar, 54

Best Plays of 1933–34, The, 137

Beyond the Horizon, 34, 38, 55, 65, 66, 67, 68, 70

Bibliography of the Works of Eugene O'Neill, 46

Birth of Tragedy, The, 5

Booth, Edwin, 12

Boulton, Agnes (see O'Neill, Agnes Boulton)

Bound East for Cardiff, 27, 30, 35, 37, 49, 53, 54, 56, 58, 60, 64, 65

Boyce, Neith, 29

Bread and Butter, 49, 53

Broom, 24

Brown, Gilmor, 116

Brown, John Mason, 102

Buddha, 153

Burns, Robert, 43

Burt, Frederick, 29, 30

By Way of Obit, 147

Call, New York, 46

Call of the Wild, The, 51

Carlin[e], Terry, 30, 32

Casa Genotta, 41, 143

Casseres, Benjamin de, 40

Chaliapin, Feodor, 148

Chapman, John, 157, 158

Chekhov, A., 36

Chris, 68, 69, 75

Chris Christopherson, 55, 68, 75

Clark, Barrett H., 124

Coleridge, S. T., 102

Commins, Saxe, vi

"Conning Tower, The," 46

Conrad, Joseph, 14, 59

Cook, George Cram, 29, 31, 35, 40

Cycle, O'Neill's, 143, 144, 145, 147, 151, 152, 161

Cyrano de Bergerac, 100

Daily News, The New York, 13, 157

Days Without End, 125, 137, 139, 140, 141, 142, 143, 151, 159

De Old Davil, 75

De Quincey, Thomas, 43

Dear Doctor, The, 26, 54

Deeter, Jasper, 9

Desire Under the Elms, 4, 63, 70, 72, 81, 87, 89, 96, 97, 98, 99, 107, 118, 123, 127, 135

Deutsch, Helen, 9
Diff'rent, 63, 79, 80, 81, 86
Dillingham, Charles, 108
Dostoievsky, F., 136
Dreamy Kid, The, 55, 63, 64
Drums of Oude, The, 72
Dynamo, 70, 83, 119, 120, 121, 122, 125, 127, 159
Dynasts, The, 117

Emperor Jones, The, 71, 72, 73, 82, 83, 160
Eugene O'Neill, a Critical Study, 140
Eugene O'Neill Returns After Twelve Years, 160
Eumenides (see Furies)
European Theories of the Drama, 124
Evening Post, The New York, 104
Exorcism, 55
Expressionism, 82, 83
"Extraordinary Story of Eugene O'Neill, The," 41

Faust, 112
Fifteen Year Record, etc., 95
First Man, The, 87, 88, 89
Fitzgerald, M. Eleanor, 9
Fog, 49, 52, 53
Fountain, The, 4, 38, 70, 87, 89, 100, 101, 102, 107, 110, 111
Free, 46
Freeman, The, 75
Freud, Siegmund, 135, 136
From Morn to Midnight, 83
Furies, The, 123, 131, 133

G.A.M., The, 54
George Pierce Baker, a Memorial, 28
Gest, Morris, 108
Ghosts, 71
Gilder, Rosamond, 152, 153, 158
Gilpin, Charles, 71, 160
Glaspell, Susan, 9, 29, 30, 31, 35
Goethe, J. W., 114
Gold, 38, 62, 63, 73, 74
Goldberg, Isaac, 9, 76
Gorky, Maxim, 22
Great God Brown, The, 4, 89, 103, 104, 105, 106, 107, 108, 110, 113, 116, 125, 127
Greek Coins, 31
Greenwich Village Theatre, 5, 38, 41, 97, 100, 103

Hairy Ape, The, 53, 82, 83, 84, 85, 86, 87, 107
Hamilton, Clayton, 26, 34
Hampden, Walter, 108
Hanau, Stella, 9
Hapgood, Hutchins, 29
Hardy, Thomas, 117
Hasenclever, Walter, 82, 84
Haunted, The, 133, 135
Heidt, Joseph, vi
Henry Miller Theatre, 139
Herald Tribune, The New York, 39, 55, 64, 84, 124
Hiawatha, 43
History of the American Drama From the Civil War to the Present Day, A, 13
Hofmannsthal, Hugo von, 75
Homecoming, 129
Honor Among the Bradleys, 55
Hopkins, Arthur, 100, 108
Hughie, 147
Hunted, The, 131

Ibsen, Henrik, 25
Iceman Cometh, The, 16, 40, 55, 63, 70, 142, 147, 151, 161
I Knew Him When—, 26
'Ile, 38, 54, 56, 61, 62, 65, 79
In the Zone, 37, 54, 56, 57, 58, 59, 60, 64
It Cannot Be Mad, 120
"It's Great When You Get In," 44

Jean-Christophe, 162
Jenkins, Kathleen, 13
Jones, Henry Arthur, 77
Jones, Robert E., 41, 64, 100
Journal of Outdoor Life, 21
Jung, Carl, 135, 136

Kahn, Otto, 103, 108, 109
Kaiser, Georg, 82, 83
Kalodyme, Louis, 15, 16
Karsner, David, 12
Kemp, Harry, 9, 23, 24, 29, 30, 31, 32, 33, 36
Kennedy, Charles O'B., 9, 83
Kenton, Edna, 9, 35
Kipling, Rudyard, 14, 43
Knock at the Door, A, 54
Komroff, Manuel, 9
Kreymborg, Alfred, 9, 24
Kropotkin, Prince, 14

Laconics, 43
Lao-Tse, 153
Last Conquest, The, 147
Latimer, Frederick P., 9, 18, 19, 24, 43
Lazarus Laughed, 5, 116, 117, 118, 119, 125, 126, 147, 148, 149
Leonardo da Vinci, 119
Lessing, G. E., 81
Letters From Greenroom Ghosts, 102
Libation-Bearers, The, 130
Life Magazine, 12
Light, James, 9, 103
Liveright, Horace, 9, 108
London, Jack, 14, 23
Long Day's Journey Into Night, 147, 154
Long Voyage Home, The, 38, 54, 56, 58, 60, 64, 65

Macgowan, Kenneth, 9, 41, 64, 100, 103, 119, 120
Madden, Richard J., 9, 68
Mantle, Burns, 137
Marco Millions, 107, 108, 109, 110, 118
Marlowe, Christopher, 102
Martin Beck Theatre, 154
Marx, Karl, 14
Mason, Walt, 43
Masses, The, 46
Memoranda on Masks, 103
Mencken, H. L., 37
Middleton, George, 60
Miller, Gilbert, 108
Moeller, Philip, 112
Mohammed, 153
Mollan, Malcolm, 20, 96
Monte Cristo, 10, 13, 17, 146
Moon of the Caribbees, etc., The, 56, 63
Moon of the Caribbees, The, 38, 45, 54, 56, 57, 58, 59, 60, 62, 63, 64, 65, 79
Moon for the Misbegotten, A, 147, 152, 154, 159, 161, 162
Mourning Becomes Electra, 72, 123, 124, 125, 126, 127-36, 149, 160
Movie Man, The, 54
Mullett, Mary B., 41

Nathan, George Jean, vi, 9, 11, 37, 38, 42, 62, 76, 77, 79, 108, 109, 142, 154
Nazimova, Alla, 25

Nicolopoulos, Basil, v
Nietzsche, Friedrich, 5, 14, 25, 84
Nobel Prize, 39
Now I Ask You, 54

O'Neill, Carlotta Monterey, vi, 8, 41, 142, 143, 145, 146, 160, 161
O'Neill, Mrs. (Agnes Boulton), 23, 40
O'Neill, Eugene, Jr., 13
O'Neill, James, 11, 12, 13, 17, 20, 21, 25, 33, 34, 49, 146
O'Neill, James, Jr., 12, 17, 84
O'Neill Lifts the Curtain on His Early Days, 15
Oresteia, 128, 132
"Out of Provincetown," 30
Overton, Grant, 56

Parsifal, 112
Pasadena Playhouse, 116
Pasley, Fred, 13, 14, 36
Pater, Walter, 119
Peakéd Hill, 32, 33, 40
Perkins, Maxwell, vi
Personal Equation, The, 26, 54
Pinero, A. W., 67
Playwrights' Theatre, 31, 36
Pleiades Club Year Book, 46
P M (New York newspaper), 152
Prideaux, Tom, 12, 18
Processional, 97
Provincetown, a Story of the Theatre, The, 9
Provincetown Players, 4, 9, 12, 31, 32, 34, 35, 37, 38, 54, 64
Provincetown Playhouse, 54, 83, 86, 102
Provincetown Plays, 37
Public Ledger, The Philadelphia, 20, 96
Pulitzer Prize, 39, 68

Quinlan, Ella (Mrs. James O'Neill), 11
Quinn, Arthur Hobson, 13

Recklessness, 49, 51, 52, 60
Rippins, The (family), 22, 25, 36
Reed, John (Jack), 30
Road to the Temple, The, 29
Robeson, Paul, 71
Robespierre, Maximilien, 144
Rogers, Will, 19
Rolland, Romain, 144
Rope, The, 55, 56, 63

Sanborn, Ralph, vi, 46
Schnitzler, Arthur, 65
Second Engineer, The, 26, 54
Service, Robert W., 43
Servitude, 53
Seven Arts Magazine, 37, 55
Shakespeare, William, 93, 114
Shay, Frank, 9, 29, 32, 35, 37, 64
Shay's Barnstormers, 64
Sheldon, Edward, 160
Shelley, Percy B., 33
Shell-shock, 55
Sixteen Authors to One, 12
Smart Set Magazine, 37, 38
Sniper, The, 54
Spoon River Anthology, 27
S.S. Glencairn, 57, 58, 64
Steele, Margaret, 29
Steele, Wilbur Daniel, 29
Stendhal, Henri Beyle, 136
Stevenson, Robert L., 116
Strange Interlude, 5, 93, 111-16, 120, 125, 127, 144, 148, 149
Straw, The, 21, 55, 69, 70, 71
Strindberg, August, 25, 64, 82, 84, 86, 115, 136
Strong, Austin, 72
Stronger, The, 64
Sun, The New York, 10, 56
Swinburne, A. C., 138

Tao House, 41, 143, 146
Telegraph, The New London, 9, 10, 18, 20, 21, 24, 43, 45, 46
Theatre Arts (Monthly; Magazine), 152, 158
Theatre Guild, vi, 9, 108, 110, 111, 112, 119, 124, 137, 139, 148, 152, 154, 162
Theatre Magazine, 30
Theatre of George Jean Nathan, The, 9, 76
They Knew What They Wanted, 97
Thirst, 33, 34, 35, 49, 50, 51, 53, 54, 56

Thirst and Other One-act Plays, etc., 33, 49, 53
Thomas, Augustus, 36
Till We Meet, 55
Times, The New York, 15, 34, 75, 78, 102, 121, 160
Toller, Ernst, 82
Tomorrow, 37
Touch of the Poet, A, 147, 151, 154, 161
Tribune, The New York, 46
Trumpet, The, 55
Tyler, George C., 38, 68

Villon, François, 43
Vorse, Mary Heaton, 29

War and Peace, 162
Warnings, 49, 51, 53, 60
Weaver, John V. A., 26
Web, The, 11, 49
Webster, Charles, 9, 17, 18
Wedekind, Frank, 25, 82, 84
Weinberger, Harry, vi
Weiss, Clara, 9
Welded, 90, 91, 92, 93, 94
Wharf Theatre, 29, 32, 34
What Price Glory?, 97
Where the Cross Is Made, 55, 56, 62, 63, 73
White Sister, The, 14
Wife for Life, A, 49
Wilde, Oscar, 116
Wilderness Edition, vi, 54, 138
Williams, John D., 38, 65
Wilson, Earl, 39, 40
Wilson, John S., 152
Wilson, Woodrow, 13
Winther, Sophus Keith, 140
Without Ending of Days, 120
Wolheim, Louis, 83
Woolf, S. J., 160
Working Notes and Extracts from a Fragmentary Work Diary, 124, 128, 134
World, The New York, 26, 71

Four manuscript sketches by O'Neill for the settings of his play, *Desire Under the Elms*. These drawings originally appeared in the Provincetown Playbill, No. 5, Season of 1924–25, from which battered source this reproduction is taken.

A CATALOGUE OF SELECTED DOVER BOOKS
IN ALL FIELDS OF INTEREST

A CATALOGUE OF SELECTED DOVER BOOKS
IN ALL FIELDS OF INTEREST

WHAT IS SCIENCE?, *N. Campbell*
The role of experiment and measurement, the function of mathematics, the nature of scientific laws, the difference between laws and theories, the limitations of science, and many similarly provocative topics are treated clearly and without technicalities by an eminent scientist. "Still an excellent introduction to scientific philosophy," H. Margenau in *Physics Today*. "A first-rate primer . . . deserves a wide audience," *Scientific American*. 192pp. 5⅜ x 8.
$$\text{S43} \qquad \text{Paperbound \$1.25}$$

THE NATURE OF LIGHT AND COLOUR IN THE OPEN AIR, *M. Minnaert*
Why are shadows sometimes blue, sometimes green, or other colors depending on the light and surroundings? What causes mirages? Why do multiple suns and moons appear in the sky? Professor Minnaert explains these unusual phenomena and hundreds of others in simple, easy-to-understand terms based on optical laws and the properties of light and color. No mathematics is required but artists, scientists, students, and everyone fascinated by these "tricks" of nature will find thousands of useful and amazing pieces of information. Hundreds of observational experiments are suggested which require no special equipment. 200 illustrations; 42 photos. xvi + 362pp. 5⅜ x 8.
$$\text{T196} \qquad \text{Paperbound \$2.00}$$

THE STRANGE STORY OF THE QUANTUM, AN ACCOUNT FOR THE GENERAL READER OF THE GROWTH OF IDEAS UNDERLYING OUR PRESENT ATOMIC KNOWLEDGE, *B. Hoffmann*
Presents lucidly and expertly, with barest amount of mathematics, the problems and theories which led to modern quantum physics. Dr. Hoffmann begins with the closing years of the 19th century, when certain trifling discrepancies were noticed, and with illuminating analogies and examples takes you through the brilliant concepts of Planck, Einstein, Pauli, Broglie, Bohr, Schroedinger, Heisenberg, Dirac, Sommerfeld, Feynman, etc. This edition includes a new, long postscript carrying the story through 1958. "Of the books attempting an account of the history and contents of our modern atomic physics which have come to my attention, this is the best," H. Margenau, Yale University, in *American Journal of Physics*. 32 tables and line illustrations. Index. 275pp. 5⅜ x 8.
$$\text{T518} \qquad \text{Paperbound \$2.00}$$

GREAT IDEAS OF MODERN MATHEMATICS: THEIR NATURE AND USE, *Jagjit Singh*
Reader with only high school math will understand main mathematical ideas of modern physics, astronomy, genetics, psychology, evolution, etc. better than many who use them as tools, but comprehend little of their basic structure. Author uses his wide knowledge of non-mathematical fields in brilliant exposition of differential equations, matrices, group theory, logic, statistics, problems of mathematical foundations, imaginary numbers, vectors, etc. Original publication. 2 appendixes. 2 indexes. 65 ills. 322pp. 5⅜ x 8.
$$\text{T587} \qquad \text{Paperbound \$2.25}$$

THE MUSIC OF THE SPHERES: THE MATERIAL UNIVERSE — FROM ATOM TO QUASAR, SIMPLY EXPLAINED, *Guy Murchie*
Vast compendium of fact, modern concept and theory, observed and calculated data, historical background guides intelligent layman through the material universe. Brilliant exposition of earth's construction, explanations for moon's craters, atmospheric components of Venus and Mars (with data from recent fly-by's), sun spots, sequences of star birth and death, neighboring galaxies, contributions of Galileo, Tycho Brahe, Kepler, etc.; and (Vol. 2) construction of the atom (describing newly discovered sigma and xi subatomic particles), theories of sound, color and light, space and time, including relativity theory, quantum theory, wave theory, probability theory, work of Newton, Maxwell, Faraday, Einstein, de Broglie, etc. "Best presentation yet offered to the intelligent general reader," *Saturday Review*. Revised (1967). Index. 319 illustrations by the author. Total of xx + 644pp. 5⅜ x 8½.
T1809, T1810 Two volume set, paperbound $4.00

FOUR LECTURES ON RELATIVITY AND SPACE, *Charles Proteus Steinmetz*
Lecture series, given by great mathematician and electrical engineer, generally considered one of the best popular-level expositions of special and general relativity theories and related questions. Steinmetz translates complex mathematical reasoning into language accessible to laymen through analogy, example and comparison. Among topics covered are relativity of motion, location, time; of mass; acceleration; 4-dimensional time-space; geometry of the gravitational field; curvature and bending of space; non-Euclidean geometry. Index. 40 illustrations. x + 142pp. 5⅜ x 8½.
S1771 Paperbound $1.35

HOW TO KNOW THE WILD FLOWERS, *Mrs. William Starr Dana*
Classic nature book that has introduced thousands to wonders of American wild flowers. Color-season principle of organization is easy to use, even by those with no botanical training, and the genial, refreshing discussions of history, folklore, uses of over 1,000 native and escape flowers, foliage plants are informative as well as fun to read. Over 170 full-page plates, collected from several editions, may be colored in to make permanent records of finds. Revised to conform with 1950 edition of Gray's Manual of Botany. xlii + 438pp. 5⅜ x 8½.
T332 Paperbound $2.25

MANUAL OF THE TREES OF NORTH AMERICA, *Charles Sprague Sargent*
Still unsurpassed as most comprehensive, reliable study of North American tree characteristics, precise locations and distribution. By dean of American dendrologists. Every tree native to U.S., Canada, Alaska; 185 genera, 717 species, described in detail—leaves, flowers, fruit, winterbuds, bark, wood, growth habits, etc. plus discussion of varieties and local variants, immaturity variations. Over 100 keys, including unusual 11-page analytical key to genera, aid in identification. 783 clear illustrations of flowers, fruit, leaves. An unmatched permanent reference work for all nature lovers. Second enlarged (1926) edition. Synopsis of families. Analytical key to genera. Glossary of technical terms. Index. 783 illustrations, 1 map. Total of 982pp. 5⅜ x 8.
T277, T278 Two volume set, paperbound $6.00

IT'S FUN TO MAKE THINGS FROM SCRAP MATERIALS,
Evelyn Glantz Hershoff
What use are empty spools, tin cans, bottle tops? What can be made from
rubber bands, clothes pins, paper clips, and buttons? This book provides
simply worded instructions and large diagrams showing you how to make
cookie cutters, toy trucks, paper turkeys, Halloween masks, telephone sets,
aprons, linoleum block- and spatter prints — in all 399 projects! Many are easy
enough for young children to figure out for themselves; some challenging
enough to entertain adults; all are remarkably ingenious ways to make things
from materials that cost pennies or less! Formerly "Scrap Fun for Everyone."
Index. 214 illustrations. 373pp. 5⅜ x 8½.   T1251   Paperbound $1.75

SYMBOLIC LOGIC and THE GAME OF LOGIC, *Lewis Carroll*
"Symbolic Logic" is not concerned with modern symbolic logic, but is instead
a collection of over 380 problems posed with charm and imagination, using
the syllogism and a fascinating diagrammatic method of drawing conclusions.
In "The Game of Logic" Carroll's whimsical imagination devises a logical game
played with 2 diagrams and counters (included) to manipulate hundreds of
tricky syllogisms. The final section, "Hit or Miss" is a lagniappe of 101 additional puzzles in the delightful Carroll manner. Until this reprint edition,
both of these books were rarities costing up to $15 each. Symbolic Logic:
Index. xxxi + 199pp. The Game of Logic: 96pp. 2 vols. bound as one. 5⅜ x 8.
                                                        T492   Paperbound $2.00

MATHEMATICAL PUZZLES OF SAM LOYD, PART I
selected and edited by M. Gardner
Choice puzzles by the greatest American puzzle creator and innovator. Selected
from his famous collection, "Cyclopedia of Puzzles," they retain the unique
style and historical flavor of the originals. There are posers based on arithmetic,
algebra, probability, game theory, route tracing, topology, counter and sliding
block, operations research, geometrical dissection. Includes the famous "14-15"
puzzle which was a national craze, and his "Horse of a Different Color" which
sold millions of copies. 117 of his most ingenious puzzles in all. 120 line
drawings and diagrams. Solutions. Selected references. xx + 167pp. 5⅜ x 8.
                                                        T498   Paperbound $1.25

STRING FIGURES AND HOW TO MAKE THEM, *Caroline Furness Jayne*
107 string figures plus variations selected from the best primitive and modern
examples developed by Navajo, Apache, pygmies of Africa, Eskimo, in Europe,
Australia, China, etc. The most readily understandable, easy-to-follow book in
English on perennially popular recreation. Crystal-clear exposition; step-by-
step diagrams. Everyone from kindergarten children to adults looking for
unusual diversion will be endlessly amused. Index. Bibliography. Introduction
by A. C. Haddon. 17 full-page plates, 960 illustrations. xxiii + 401pp. 5⅜ x 8½
                                                        T152   Paperbound $2.25

PAPER FOLDING FOR BEGINNERS, *W. D. Murray and F. J. Rigney*
A delightful introduction to the varied and entertaining Japanese art of
origami (paper folding), with a full, crystal-clear text that anticipates every
difficulty; over 275 clearly labeled diagrams of all important stages in creation.
You get results at each stage, since complex figures are logically developed
from simpler ones. 43 different pieces are explained: sailboats, frogs, roosters,
etc. 6 photographic plates. 279 diagrams. 95pp. 5⅝ x 8⅜.
                                                        T713   Paperbound $1.00

PRINCIPLES OF ART HISTORY,
H. Wölfflin
Analyzing such terms as "baroque," "classic," "neoclassic," "primitive,"
"picturesque," and 164 different works by artists like Botticelli, van Cleve,
Dürer, Hobbema, Holbein, Hals, Rembrandt, Titian, Brueghel, Vermeer, and
many others, the author establishes the classifications of art history and style
on a firm, concrete basis. This classic of art criticism shows what really
occurred between the 14th-century primitives and the sophistication of the
18th century in terms of basic attitudes and philosophies. "A remarkable
lesson in the art of seeing," *Sat. Rev. of Literature.* Translated from the 7th
German edition. 150 illustrations. 254pp. 6⅛ x 9¼. T276 Paperbound $2.00

PRIMITIVE ART,
Franz Boas
This authoritative and exhaustive work by a great American anthropologist
covers the entire gamut of primitive art. Pottery, leatherwork, metal work,
stone work, wood, basketry, are treated in detail. Theories of primitive art,
historical depth in art history, technical virtuosity, unconscious levels of patterning, symbolism, styles, literature, music, dance, etc. A must book for the
interested layman, the anthropologist, artist, handicrafter (hundreds of unusual motifs), and the historian. Over 900 illustrations (50 ceramic vessels,
12 totem poles, etc.). 376pp. 5⅜ x 8.   T25   Paperbound $2.50

THE GENTLEMAN AND CABINET MAKER'S DIRECTOR,
Thomas Chippendale
A reprint of the 1762 catalogue of furniture designs that went on to influence
generations of English and Colonial and Early Republic American furniture
makers. The 200 plates, most of them full-page sized, show Chippendale's
designs for French (Louis XV), Gothic, and Chinese-manner chairs, sofas,
canopy and dome beds, cornices, chamber organs, cabinets, shaving tables,
commodes, picture frames, frets, candle stands, chimney pieces, decorations, etc.
The drawings are all elegant and highly detailed; many include construction
diagrams and elevations. A supplement of 24 photographs shows surviving
pieces of original and Chippendale-style pieces of furniture. Brief biography
of Chippendale by N. I. Bienenstock, editor of *Furniture World.* Reproduced
from the 1762 edition. 200 plates, plus 19 photographic plates. vi + 249pp.
9⅛ x 12¼.   T1601   Paperbound $3.50

AMERICAN ANTIQUE FURNITURE: A BOOK FOR AMATEURS,
Edgar G. Miller, Jr.
Standard introduction and practical guide to identification of valuable
American antique furniture. 2115 illustrations, mostly photographs taken by
the author in 148 private homes, are arranged in chronological order in extensive chapters on chairs, sofas, chests, desks, bedsteads, mirrors, tables, clocks,
and other articles. Focus is on furniture accessible to the collector, including
simpler pieces and a larger than usual coverage of Empire style. Introductory
chapters identify structural elements, characteristics of various styles, how to
avoid fakes, etc. "We are frequently asked to name some book on American
furniture that will meet the requirements of the novice collector, the beginning dealer, and . . . the general public. . . . We believe Mr. Miller's two
volumes more completely satisfy this specification than any other work,"
Antiques. Appendix. Index. Total of vi + 1106pp. 7⅞ x 10¾.
                       T1599, T1600   Two volume set, paperbound $7.50

THE BAD CHILD'S BOOK OF BEASTS, MORE BEASTS FOR WORSE CHILDREN, and A MORAL ALPHABET, *H. Belloc*
Hardly and anthology of humorous verse has appeared in the last 50 years without at least a couple of these famous nonsense verses. But one must see the entire volumes — with all the delightful original illustrations by Sir Basil Blackwood — to appreciate fully Belloc's charming and witty verses that play so subacidly on the platitudes of life and morals that beset his day — and ours. A great humor classic. Three books in one. Total of 157pp. 5⅜ x 8.
T749   Paperbound $1.00

THE DEVIL'S DICTIONARY, *Ambrose Bierce*
Sardonic and irreverent barbs puncturing the pomposities and absurdities of American politics, business, religion, literature, and arts, by the country's greatest satirist in the classic tradition. Epigrammatic as Shaw, piercing as Swift, American as Mark Twain, Will Rogers, and Fred Allen, Bierce will always remain the favorite of a small coterie of enthusiasts, and of writers and speakers whom he supplies with "some of the most gorgeous witticisms of the English language" (H. L. Mencken). Over 1000 entries in alphabetical order. 144pp. 5⅜ x 8.   T487   Paperbound $1.00

THE COMPLETE NONSENSE OF EDWARD LEAR.
This is the only complete edition of this master of gentle madness available at a popular price. *A Book of Nonsense, Nonsense Songs, More Nonsense Songs and Stories* in their entirety with all the old favorites that have delighted children and adults for years. The Dong With A Luminous Nose, The Jumblies, The Owl and the Pussycat, and hundreds of other bits of wonderful nonsense: 214 limericks, 3 sets of Nonsense Botany, 5 Nonsense Alphabets, 546 drawings by Lear himself, and much more. 320pp. 5⅜ x 8.   T167   Paperbound $1.75

THE WIT AND HUMOR OF OSCAR WILDE, *ed. by Alvin Redman*
Wilde at his most brilliant, in 1000 epigrams exposing weaknesses and hypocrisies of "civilized" society. Divided into 49 categories—sin, wealth, women, America, etc.—to aid writers, speakers. Includes excerpts from his trials, books, plays, criticism. Formerly "The Epigrams of Oscar Wilde." Introduction by Vyvyan Holland, Wilde's only living son. Introductory essay by editor. 260pp. 5⅜ x 8.   T602   Paperbound $1.50

A CHILD'S PRIMER OF NATURAL HISTORY, *Oliver Herford*
Scarcely an anthology of whimsy and humor has appeared in the last 50 years without a contribution from Oliver Herford. Yet the works from which these examples are drawn have been almost impossible to obtain! Here at last are Herford's improbable definitions of a menagerie of familiar and weird animals, each verse illustrated by the author's own drawings. 24 drawings in 2 colors; 24 additional drawings. vii + 95pp. 6½ x 6.   T1647   Paperbound $1.00

THE BROWNIES: THEIR BOOK, *Palmer Cox*
The book that made the Brownies a household word. Generations of readers have enjoyed the antics, predicaments and adventures of these jovial sprites, who emerge from the forest at night to play or to come to the aid of a deserving human. Delightful illustrations by the author decorate nearly every page. 24 short verse tales with 266 illustrations. 155pp. 6⅝ x 9¼.
T1265   Paperbound $1.50

THE PRINCIPLES OF PSYCHOLOGY,
William James

The full long-course, unabridged, of one of the great classics of Western literature and science. Wonderfully lucid descriptions of human mental activity, the stream of thought, consciousness, time perception, memory, imagination, emotions, reason, abnormal phenomena, and similar topics. Original contributions are integrated with the work of such men as Berkeley, Binet, Mills, Darwin, Hume, Kant, Royce, Schopenhauer, Spinoza, Locke, Descartes, Galton, Wundt, Lotze, Herbart, Fechner, and scores of others. All contrasting interpretations of mental phenomena are examined in detail—introspective analysis, philosophical interpretation, and experimental research. "A classic," *Journal of Consulting Psychology*. "The main lines are as valid as ever," *Psychoanalytical Quarterly*. "Standard reading . . . a classic of interpretation," *Psychiatric Quarterly*. 94 illustrations. 1408pp. 5⅜ x 8.

T381, T382 Two volume set, paperbound $6.00

VISUAL ILLUSIONS: THEIR CAUSES, CHARACTERISTICS AND APPLICATIONS,
M. Luckiesh

"Seeing is deceiving," asserts the author of this introduction to virtually every type of optical illusion known. The text both describes and explains the principles involved in color illusions, figure-ground, distance illusions, etc. 100 photographs, drawings and diagrams prove how easy it is to fool the sense: circles that aren't round, parallel lines that seem to bend, stationary figures that seem to move as you stare at them — illustration after illustration strains our credulity at what we see. Fascinating book from many points of view, from applications for artists, in camouflage, etc. to the psychology of vision. New introduction by William Ittleson, Dept. of Psychology, Queens College. Index. Bibliography. xxi + 252pp. 5⅜ x 8½. T1530 Paperbound $1.50

FADS AND FALLACIES IN THE NAME OF SCIENCE,
Martin Gardner

This is the standard account of various cults, quack systems, and delusions which have masqueraded as science: hollow earth fanatics. Reich and orgone sex energy, dianetics, Atlantis, multiple moons, Forteanism, flying saucers, medical fallacies like iridiagnosis, zone therapy, etc. A new chapter has been added on Bridey Murphy, psionics, and other recent manifestations in this field. This is a fair, reasoned appraisal of eccentric theory which provides excellent inoculation against cleverly masked nonsense. "Should be read by everyone, scientist and non-scientist alike," R. T. Birge, Prof. Emeritus of Physics, Univ. of California; Former President, American Physical Society. Index. x + 365pp. 5⅜ x 8. T394 Paperbound $2.00

ILLUSIONS AND DELUSIONS OF THE SUPERNATURAL AND THE OCCULT,
D. H. Rawcliffe

Holds up to rational examination hundreds of persistent delusions including crystal gazing, automatic writing, table turning, mediumistic trances, mental healing, stigmata, lycanthropy, live burial, the Indian Rope Trick, spiritualism, dowsing, telepathy, clairvoyance, ghosts, ESP, etc. The author explains and exposes the mental and physical deceptions involved, making this not only an exposé of supernatural phenomena, but a valuable exposition of characteristic types of abnormal psychology. Originally titled "The Psychology of the Occult." 14 illustrations. Index. 551pp. 5⅜ x 8. T503 Paperbound $2.75

FAIRY TALE COLLECTIONS, *edited by Andrew Lang*
Andrew Lang's fairy tale collections make up the richest shelf-full of traditional children's stories anywhere available. Lang supervised the translation of stories from all over the world—familiar European tales collected by Grimm, animal stories from Negro Africa, myths of primitive Australia, stories from Russia, Hungary, Iceland, Japan, and many other countries. Lang's selection of translations are unusually high; many authorities consider that the most familiar tales find their best versions in these volumes. All collections are richly decorated and illustrated by H. J. Ford and other artists.

THE BLUE FAIRY BOOK. 37 stories. 138 illustrations. ix + 390pp. 5⅜ x 8½.
T1437 Paperbound $1.95

THE GREEN FAIRY BOOK. 42 stories. 100 illustrations. xiii + 366pp. 5⅜ x 8½.
T1439 Paperbound $1.75

THE BROWN FAIRY BOOK. 32 stories. 50 illustrations, 8 in color. xii + 350pp. 5⅜ x 8½.
T1438 Paperbound $1.95

THE BEST TALES OF HOFFMANN, *edited by E. F. Bleiler*
10 stories by E. T. A. Hoffmann, one of the greatest of all writers of fantasy. The tales include "The Golden Flower Pot," "Automata," "A New Year's Eve Adventure," "Nutcracker and the King of Mice," "Sand-Man," and others. Vigorous characterizations of highly eccentric personalities, remarkably imaginative situations, and intensely fast pacing has made these tales popular all over the world for 150 years. Editor's introduction. 7 drawings by Hoffmann. xxxiii + 419pp. 5⅜ x 8½.
T1793 Paperbound $2.25

GHOST AND HORROR STORIES OF AMBROSE BIERCE, *edited by E. F. Bleiler*
Morbid, eerie, horrifying tales of possessed poets, shabby aristocrats, revived corpses, and haunted malefactors. Widely acknowledged as the best of their kind between Poe and the moderns, reflecting their author's inner torment and bitter view of life. Includes "Damned Thing," "The Middle Toe of the Right Foot," "The Eyes of the Panther," "Visions of the Night," "Moxon's Master," and over a dozen others. Editor's introduction. xxii + 199pp. 5⅜ x 8½.
T767 Paperbound $1.50

THREE GOTHIC NOVELS, *edited by E. F. Bleiler*
Originators of the still popular Gothic novel form, influential in ushering in early 19th-century Romanticism. Horace Walpole's *Castle of Otranto*, William Beckford's *Vathek*, John Polidori's *The Vampyre*, and a *Fragment* by Lord Byron are enjoyable as exciting reading or as documents in the history of English literature. Editor's introduction. xi + 291pp. 5⅜ x 8½.
T1232 Paperbound $2.00

BEST GHOST STORIES OF LEFANU, *edited by E. F. Bleiler*
Though admired by such critics as V. S. Pritchett, Charles Dickens and Henry James, ghost stories by the Irish novelist Joseph Sheridan LeFanu have never become as widely known as his detective fiction. About half of the 16 stories in this collection have never before been available in America. Collection includes "Carmilla" (perhaps the best vampire story ever written), "The Haunted Baronet," "The Fortunes of Sir Robert Ardagh," and the classic "Green Tea." Editor's introduction. 7 contemporary illustrations. Portrait of LeFanu. xii + 467pp. 5⅜ x 8.
T415 Paperbound $2.50

EASY-TO-DO ENTERTAINMENTS AND DIVERSIONS WITH COINS, CARDS, STRING, PAPER AND MATCHES, *R. M. Abraham*

Over 300 tricks, games and puzzles will provide young readers with absorbing fun. Sections on card games; paper-folding; tricks with coins, matches and pieces of string; games for the agile; toy-making from common household objects; mathematical recreations; and 50 miscellaneous pastimes. Anyone in charge of groups of youngsters, including hard-pressed parents, and in need of suggestions on how to keep children sensibly amused and quietly content will find this book indispensable. Clear, simple text, copious number of delightful line drawings and illustrative diagrams. Originally titled "Winter Nights' Entertainments." Introduction by Lord Baden Powell. 329 illustrations. v + 186pp. 5⅜ x 8½. T921 Paperbound $1.00

AN INTRODUCTION TO CHESS MOVES AND TACTICS SIMPLY EXPLAINED, *Leonard Barden*

Beginner's introduction to the royal game. Names, possible moves of the pieces, definitions of essential terms, how games are won, etc. explained in 30-odd pages. With this background you'll be able to sit right down and play. Balance of book teaches strategy — openings, middle game, typical endgame play, and suggestions for improving your game. A sample game is fully analyzed. True middle-level introduction, teaching you all the essentials without oversimplifying or losing you in a maze of detail. 58 figures. 102pp. 5⅜ x 8½. T1210 Paperbound $1.25

LASKER'S MANUAL OF CHESS, *Dr. Emanuel Lasker*

Probably the greatest chess player of modern times, Dr. Emanuel Lasker held the world championship 28 years, independent of passing schools or fashions. This unmatched study of the game, chiefly for intermediate to skilled players, analyzes basic methods, combinations, position play, the aesthetics of chess, dozens of different openings, etc., with constant reference to great modern games. Contains a brilliant exposition of Steinitz's important theories. Introduction by Fred Reinfeld. Tables of Lasker's tournament record. 3 indices. 308 diagrams. 1 photograph. xxx + 349pp. 5⅜ x 8. T640 Paperbound $2.50

COMBINATIONS: THE HEART OF CHESS, *Irving Chernev*

Step-by-step from simple combinations to complex, this book, by a well-known chess writer, shows you the intricacies of pins, counter-pins, knight forks, and smothered mates. Other chapters show alternate lines of play to those taken in actual championship games; boomerang combinations; classic examples of brilliant combination play by Nimzovich, Rubinstein, Tarrasch, Botvinnik, Alekhine and Capablanca. Index. 356 diagrams. ix + 245pp. 5⅜ x 8½. T1744 Paperbound $2.00

HOW TO SOLVE CHESS PROBLEMS, *K. S. Howard*

Full of practical suggestions for the fan or the beginner — who knows only the moves of the chessmen. Contains preliminary section and 58 two-move, 46 three-move, and 8 four-move problems composed by 27 outstanding American problem creators in the last 30 years. Explanation of all terms and exhaustive index. "Just what is wanted for the student," Brian Harley. 112 problems, solutions. vi + 171pp. 5⅜ x 8. T748 Paperbound $1.35

SOCIAL THOUGHT FROM LORE TO SCIENCE,
H. E. Barnes and H. Becker
An immense survey of sociological thought and ways of viewing, studying, planning, and reforming society from earliest times to the present. Includes thought on society of preliterate peoples, ancient non-Western cultures, and every great movement in Europe, America, and modern Japan. Analyzes hundreds of great thinkers: Plato, Augustine, Bodin, Vico, Montesquieu, Herder, Comte, Marx, etc. Weighs the contributions of utopians, sophists, fascists and communists; economists, jurists, philosophers, ecclesiastics, and every 19th and 20th century school of scientific sociology, anthropology, and social psychology throughout the world. Combines topical, chronological, and regional approaches, treating the evolution of social thought as a process rather than as a series of mere topics. "Impressive accuracy, competence, and discrimination . . . easily the best single survey," *Nation.* Thoroughly revised, with new material up to 1960. 2 indexes. Over 2200 bibliographical notes. Three volume set. Total of 1586pp. 5⅜ x 8.

T901, T902, T903   Three volume set, paperbound $9.00

A HISTORY OF HISTORICAL WRITING, *Harry Elmer Barnes*
Virtually the only adequate survey of the whole course of historical writing in a single volume. Surveys developments from the beginnings of historiography in the ancient Near East and the Classical World, up through the Cold War. Covers major historians in detail, shows interrelationship with cultural background, makes clear individual contributions, evaluates and estimates importance; also enormously rich upon minor authors and thinkers who are usually passed over. Packed with scholarship and learning, clear, easily written. Indispensable to every student of history. Revised and enlarged up to 1961. Index and bibliography. xv + 442pp. 5⅜ x 8½.

T104   Paperbound $2.50

JOHANN SEBASTIAN BACH, *Philipp Spitta*
The complete and unabridged text of the definitive study of Bach. Written some 70 years ago, it is still unsurpassed for its coverage of nearly all aspects of Bach's life and work. There could hardly be a finer non-technical introduction to Bach's music than the detailed, lucid analyses which Spitta provides for hundreds of individual pieces. 26 solid pages are devoted to the B minor mass, for example, and 30 pages to the glorious St. Matthew Passion. This monumental set also includes a major analysis of the music of the 18th century: Buxtehude, Pachelbel, etc. "Unchallenged as the last word on one of the supreme geniuses of music," John Barkham, *Saturday Review Syndicate.* Total of 1819pp. Heavy cloth binding. 5⅜ x 8.

T252   Two volume set, clothbound $15.00

BEETHOVEN AND HIS NINE SYMPHONIES, *George Grove*
In this modern middle-level classic of musicology Grove not only analyzes all nine of Beethoven's symphonies very thoroughly in terms of their musical structure, but also discusses the circumstances under which they were written, Beethoven's stylistic development, and much other background material. This is an extremely rich book, yet very easily followed; it is highly recommended to anyone seriously interested in music. Over 250 musical passages. Index. viii + 407pp. 5⅜ x 8.

T334   Paperbound $2.25

CATALOGUE OF DOVER BOOKS

THREE SCIENCE FICTION NOVELS,
John Taine

Acknowledged by many as the best SF writer of the 1920's, Taine (under the name Eric Temple Bell) was also a Professor of Mathematics of considerable renown. Reprinted here are *The Time Stream*, generally considered Taine's best, *The Greatest Game*, a biological-fiction novel, and *The Purple Sapphire*, involving a supercivilization of the past. Taine's stories tie fantastic narratives to frameworks of original and logical scientific concepts. Speculation is often profound on such questions as the nature of time, concept of entropy, cyclical universes, etc. 4 contemporary illustrations. v + 532pp. 5⅜ x 8⅜.

T1180   Paperbound $2.00

SEVEN SCIENCE FICTION NOVELS,
H. G. Wells

Full unabridged texts of 7 science-fiction novels of the master. Ranging from biology, physics, chemistry, astronomy, to sociology and other studies, Mr. Wells extrapolates whole worlds of strange and intriguing character. "One will have to go far to match this for entertainment, excitement, and sheer pleasure . . ."*New York Times*. Contents: The Time Machine, The Island of Dr. Moreau, The First Men in the Moon, The Invisible Man, The War of the Worlds, The Food of the Gods, In The Days of the Comet. 1015pp. 5⅜ x 8.

T264   Clothbound $5.00

28 SCIENCE FICTION STORIES OF H. G. WELLS.

Two full, unabridged novels, *Men Like Gods* and *Star Begotten*, plus 26 short stories by the master science-fiction writer of all time! Stories of space, time, invention, exploration, futuristic adventure. Partial contents: *The Country of the Blind, In the Abyss, The Crystal Egg, The Man Who Could Work Miracles, A Story of Days to Come, The Empire of the Ants, The Magic Shop, The Valley of the Spiders, A Story of the Stone Age, Under the Knife, Sea Raiders*, etc. An indispensable collection for the library of anyone interested in science fiction adventure. 928pp. 5⅜ x 8.

T265   Clothbound $5.00

THREE MARTIAN NOVELS,
Edgar Rice Burroughs

Complete, unabridged reprinting, in one volume, of Thuvia, Maid of Mars; Chessmen of Mars; The Master Mind of Mars. Hours of science-fiction adventure by a modern master storyteller. Reset in large clear type for easy reading. 16 illustrations by J. Allen St. John. vi + 490pp. 5⅜ x 8½.

T39   Paperbound $2.50

AN INTELLECTUAL AND CULTURAL HISTORY OF THE WESTERN WORLD,
Harry Elmer Barnes

Monumental 3-volume survey of intellectual development of Europe from primitive cultures to the present day. Every significant product of human intellect traced through history: art, literature, mathematics, physical sciences, medicine, music, technology, social sciences, religions, jurisprudence, education, etc. Presentation is lucid and specific, analyzing in detail specific discoveries, theories, literary works, and so on. Revised (1965) by recognized scholars in specialized fields under the direction of Prof. Barnes. Revised bibliography. Indexes. 24 illustrations. Total of xxix + 1318pp.

T1275, T1276, T1277   Three volume set, paperbound $7.50

HEAR ME TALKIN' TO YA, *edited by Nat Shapiro and Nat Hentoff*
In their own words, Louis Armstrong, King Oliver, Fletcher Henderson, Bunk Johnson, Bix Beiderbecke, Billy Holiday, Fats Waller, Jelly Roll Morton, Duke Ellington, and many others comment on the origins of jazz in New Orleans and its growth in Chicago's South Side, Kansas City's jam sessions, Depression Harlem, and the modernism of the West Coast schools. Taken from taped conversations, letters, magazine articles, other first-hand sources. Editors' introduction. xvi + 429pp. 5⅜ x 8½.   T1726   Paperbound $2.00

THE JOURNAL OF HENRY D. THOREAU
A 25-year record by the great American observer and critic, as complete a record of a great man's inner life as is anywhere available. Thoreau's Journals served him as raw material for his formal pieces, as a place where he could develop his ideas, as an outlet for his interests in wild life and plants, in writing as an art, in classics of literature, Walt Whitman and other contemporaries, in politics, slavery, individual's relation to the State, etc. The Journals present a portrait of a remarkable man, and are an observant social history. Unabridged republication of 1906 edition, Bradford Torrey and Francis H. Allen, editors. Illustrations. Total of 1888pp. 8⅜ x 12¼.
                        T312, T313   Two volume set, clothbound $25.00

A SHAKESPEARIAN GRAMMAR, *E. A. Abbott*
Basic reference to Shakespeare and his contemporaries, explaining through thousands of quotations from Shakespeare, Jonson, Beaumont and Fletcher, North's *Plutarch* and other sources the grammatical usage differing from the modern. First published in 1870 and written by a scholar who spent much of his life isolating principles of Elizabethan language, the book is unlikely ever to be superseded. Indexes. xxiv + 511pp. 5⅜ x 8½. T1582 Paperbound $2.75

FOLK-LORE OF SHAKESPEARE, *T. F. Thistelton Dyer*
Classic study, drawing from Shakespeare a large body of references to supernatural beliefs, terminology of falconry and hunting, games and sports, good luck charms, marriage customs, folk medicines, superstitions about plants, animals, birds, argot of the underworld, sexual slang of London, proverbs, drinking customs, weather lore, and much else. From full compilation comes a mirror of the 17th-century popular mind. Index. ix + 526pp. 5⅜ x 8½.
                                T1614   Paperbound $2.75

THE NEW VARIORUM SHAKESPEARE, *edited by H. H. Furness*
By far the richest editions of the plays ever produced in any country or language. Each volume contains complete text (usually First Folio) of the play, all variants in Quarto and other Folio texts, editorial changes by every major editor to Furness's own time (1900), footnotes to obscure references or language, extensive quotes from literature of Shakespearian criticism, essays on plot sources (often reprinting sources in full), and much more.

HAMLET, *edited by H. H. Furness*
Total of xxvi + 905pp. 5⅜ x 8½.
                        T1004, T1005   Two volume set, paperbound $5.25

TWELFTH NIGHT, *edited by H. H. Furness*
Index. xxii + 434pp. 5⅜ x 8½.   T1189   Paperbound $2.75

La Boheme by Giacomo Puccini,
translated and introduced by Ellen H. Bleiler
Complete handbook for the operagoer, with everything needed for full enjoy-
ment except the musical score itself. Complete Italian libretto, with new,
modern English line-by-line translation—the only libretto printing all repeats;
biography of Puccini; the librettists; background to the opera, Murger's La
Boheme, etc.; circumstances of composition and performances; plot summary;
and pictorial section of 73 illustrations showing Puccini, famous singers and
performances, etc. Large clear type for easy reading. 124pp. 5⅜ x 8½.
T404 Paperbound $1.25

Antonio Stradivari: His Life and Work (1644-1737),
W. Henry Hill, Arthur F. Hill, and Alfred E. Hill
Still the only book that really delves into life and art of the incomparable
Italian craftsman, maker of the finest musical instruments in the world today.
The authors, expert violin-makers themselves, discuss Stradivari's ancestry, his
construction and finishing techniques, distinguished characteristics of many
of his instruments and their locations. Included, too, is story of introduction
of his instruments into France, England, first revelation of their supreme
merit, and information on his labels, number of instruments made, prices,
mystery of ingredients of his varnish, tone of pre-1684 Stradivari violin and
changes between 1684 and 1690. An extremely interesting, informative account
for all music lovers, from craftsman to concert-goer. Republication of original
(1902) edition. New introduction by Sydney Beck, Head of Rare Book and
Manuscript Collections, Music Division, New York Public Library. Analytical
index by Rembert Wurlitzer. Appendixes. 68 illustrations. 30 full-page plates.
4 in color. xxvi + 315pp. 5⅜ x 8½. T425 Paperbound $2.25

Musical Autographs from Monteverdi to Hindemith,
Emanuel Winternitz
For beauty, for intrinsic interest, for perspective on the composer's personality,
for subtleties of phrasing, shading, emphasis indicated in the autograph but
suppressed in the printed score, the mss. of musical composition are fascinating
documents which repay close study in many different ways. This 2-volume
work reprints facsimiles of mss. by virtually every major composer, and many
minor figures—196 examples in all. A full text points out what can be learned
from mss., analyzes each sample. Index. Bibliography. 18 figures. 196 plates.
Total of 170pp. of text. 7⅞ x 10¾.
T1312, T1313 Two volume set, paperbound $5.00

J. S. Bach,
Albert Schweitzer
One of the few great full-length studies of Bach's life and work, and the
study upon which Schweitzer's renown as a musicologist rests. On first appearance (1911), revolutionized Bach performance. The only writer on Bach to
be musicologist, performing musician, and student of history, theology and
philosophy, Schweitzer contributes particularly full sections on history of German Protestant church music, theories on motivic pictorial representations
in vocal music, and practical suggestions for performance. Translated by
Ernest Newman. Indexes. 5 illustrations. 650 musical examples. Total of xix
+ 928pp. 5⅜ x 8½. T1631, T1632 Two volume set, paperbound $4.50

THE METHODS OF ETHICS, *Henry Sidgwick*
Propounding no organized system of its own, study subjects every major methodological approach to ethics to rigorous, objective analysis. Study discusses and relates ethical thought of Plato, Aristotle, Bentham, Clarke, Butler, Hobbes, Hume, Mill, Spencer, Kant, and dozens of others. Sidgwick retains conclusions from each system which follow from ethical premises, rejecting the faulty. Considered by many in the field to be among the most important treatises on ethical philosophy. Appendix. Index. xlvii + 528pp. 5⅜ x 8½.
T1608 Paperbound $2.50

TEUTONIC MYTHOLOGY, *Jakob Grimm*
A milestone in Western culture; the work which established on a modern basis the study of history of religions and comparative religions. 4-volume work assembles and interprets everything available on religious and folkloristic beliefs of Germanic people (including Scandinavians, Anglo-Saxons, etc.). Assembling material from such sources as Tacitus, surviving Old Norse and Icelandic texts, archeological remains, folktales, surviving superstitions, comparative traditions, linguistic analysis, etc. Grimm explores pagan deities, heroes, folklore of nature, religious practices, and every other area of pagan German belief. To this day, the unrivaled, definitive, exhaustive study. Translated by J. S. Stallybrass from 4th (1883) German edition. Indexes. Total of lxxvii + 1887pp. 5⅜ x 8½.
T1602, T1603, T1604, T1605 Four volume set, paperbound $11.00

THE I CHING, *translated by James Legge*
Called "The Book of Changes" in English, this is one of the Five Classics edited by Confucius, basic and central to Chinese thought. Explains perhaps the most complex system of divination known, founded on the theory that all things happening at any one time have characteristic features which can be isolated and related. Significant in Oriental studies, in history of religions and philosophy, and also to Jungian psychoanalysis and other areas of modern European thought. Index. Appendixes. 6 plates. xxi + 448pp. 5⅜ x 8½.
T1062 Paperbound $2.75

HISTORY OF ANCIENT PHILOSOPHY, *W. Windelband*
One of the clearest, most accurate comprehensive surveys of Greek and Roman philosophy. Discusses ancient philosophy in general, intellectual life in Greece in the 7th and 6th centuries B.C., Thales, Anaximander, Anaximenes, Heraclitus, the Eleatics, Empedocles, Anaxagoras, Leucippus, the Pythagoreans, the Sophists, Socrates, Democritus (20 pages), Plato (50 pages), Aristotle (70 pages), the Peripatetics, Stoics, Epicureans, Sceptics, Neo-platonists, Christian Apologists, etc. 2nd German edition translated by H. E. Cushman. xv + 393pp. 5⅜ x 8.
T357 Paperbound $2.25

THE PALACE OF PLEASURE, *William Painter*
Elizabethan versions of Italian and French novels from *The Decameron*, Cinthio, Straparola, Queen Margaret of Navarre, and other continental sources — the very work that provided Shakespeare and dozens of his contemporaries with many of their plots and sub-plots and, therefore, justly considered one of the most influential books in all English literature. It is also a book that any reader will still enjoy. Total of cviii + 1,224pp.
T1691, T1692, T1693 Three volume set, paperbound $6.75

THE WONDERFUL WIZARD OF OZ, *L. F. Baum*
All the original W. W. Denslow illustrations in full color—as much a part of
"The Wizard" as Tenniel's drawings are of "Alice in Wonderland." "The
Wizard" is still America's best-loved fairy tale, in which, as the author expresses
it, "The wonderment and joy are retained and the heartaches and nightmares
left out." Now today's young readers can enjoy every word and wonderful picture of the original book. New introduction by Martin Gardner. A Baum
bibliography. 23 full-page color plates. viii + 268pp. 5⅜ x 8.
T691 Paperbound $1.75

THE MARVELOUS LAND OF OZ, *L. F. Baum*
This is the equally enchanting sequel to the "Wizard," continuing the adventures of the Scarecrow and the Tin Woodman. The hero this time is a little
boy named Tip, and all the delightful Oz magic is still present. This is the
Oz book with the Animated Saw-Horse, the Woggle-Bug, and Jack Pumpkin-
head. All the original John R. Neill illustrations, 10 in full color. 287pp.
5⅜ x 8.
T692 Paperbound $1.75

ALICE'S ADVENTURES UNDER GROUND, *Lewis Carroll*
The original *Alice in Wonderland*, hand-lettered and illustrated by Carroll
himself, and originally presented as a Christmas gift to a child-friend. Adults
as well as children will enjoy this charming volume, reproduced faithfully
in this Dover edition. While the story is essentially the same, there are slight
changes, and Carroll's spritely drawings present an intriguing alternative to
the famous Tenniel illustrations. One of the most popular books in Dover's
catalogue. Introduction by Martin Gardner. 38 illustrations. 128pp. 5⅜ x 8½.
T1482 Paperbound $1.00

THE NURSERY "ALICE," *Lewis Carroll*
While most of us consider *Alice in Wonderland* a story for children of all
ages, Carroll himself felt it was beyond younger children. He therefore provided this simplified version, illustrated with the famous Tenniel drawings
enlarged and colored in delicate tints, for children aged "from Nought to
Five." Dover's edition of this now rare classic is a faithful copy of the 1889
printing, including 20 illustrations by Tenniel, and front and back covers
reproduced in full color. Introduction by Martin Gardner. xxiii + 67pp.
6⅛ x 9¼.
T1610 Paperbound $1.75

THE STORY OF KING ARTHUR AND HIS KNIGHTS, *Howard Pyle*
A fast-paced, exciting retelling of the best known Arthurian legends for young
readers by one of America's best story tellers and illustrators. The sword
Excalibur, wooing of Guinevere, Merlin and his downfall, adventures of Sir
Pellias and Gawaine, and others. The pen and ink illustrations are vividly
imagined and wonderfully drawn. 41 illustrations. xviii + 313pp. 6⅛ x 9¼.
T1445 Paperbound $1.75

Prices subject to change without notice.